Breaking
DEMONIC
CYCLES
FROM THE
COURTS OF HEAVEN

DESTINY IMAGE BOOKS BY ROBERT HENDERSON

Breaking DEMONIC CYCLES

FROM THE
COURTS OF HEAVEN

Step Into Your New Season Now!

ROBERT HENDERSON

DESTINY IMAGE® PUBLISHERS, INC.

PO Box 310, Shippensburg, PA 17257-0310

"Publishing cutting-edge prophetic resources to supernaturally empower the body of Christ"

This book and all other Destiny Image and Destiny Image Fiction books are available at Christian bookstores and distributors worldwide.

For more information on foreign distributors, call 717-532-3040.

Reach us on the Internet: www.destinyimage.com.

ISBN 13 TP: 978-0-7684-7548-7
ISBN 13 eBook: 978-0-7684-7549-4

For Worldwide Distribution, Printed in the USA
1 2 3 4 5 6 7 8 / 28 27 26 25 24

Contents

CHAPTER 1

Getting Unstuck

God likes new things. He even says in His word that He makes everything new. Revelation 21:4-5 gives us the promise that the old times of sorrow will be replaced with new times of rejoicing.

And God will wipe away every tear from their eyes; there shall be no more death, nor sorrow, nor crying. There shall be no more pain, for the former things have passed away. Then He who sat on the throne said, "Behold, I make all things new." And He said to me, "Write, for these words are true and faithful."

Of course, this is a promise of the life that we will have in eternity. Yet it does display God's passion now to bring us from the old and into the new. It's really interesting that the old is attached to death, sorrow, crying, and pain. We all know these experiences very well. Yet it is the desire and longing of God to move us from these troublesome times and into a fresh, new life in Jesus. We are told in 2 Corinthians 5:16-17 that right now we are to be a new creation.

Therefore, from now on, we regard no one according to the flesh. Even though we have known Christ according to the flesh, yet now we know Him thus no longer. Therefore, if anyone is in Christ, he is a new creation; old things have passed away; behold, all things have become new.

This scripture would seem to imply that the new thing God makes us into will be very different from the old. Paul says that as we are transformed by the Lord, we become unrecognizable compared to what we once were. In fact, the new thing God turns us into is not a simple renewing of the old, but actually a brand-new expression of something not seen before. Therefore, what we once were does not exist anymore. We are a new creation. We are a new species that expresses the handiwork of our loving God. This is what Ephesians 2:10 tells us. We are His workmanship that has been designed and created by Him.

For we are His workmanship, created in Christ Jesus for good works, which God prepared beforehand that we should walk in them.

The word *workmanship* is the Greek word *poiema*. It is where our English word *poem* comes from. It actually means "a product or thing that is made." It implies a *work of art*. We are God's work of art and He is our artist. We are filled with His creativity and ingenuity. Anytime we view or encounter a work of art, we are encountering the character and person of the artist. God intends for us to be an expression of who He is into the earth. Just like a painting manifests the artist's state of mind and communicates their passion, so are we to express God's heart.

Remember that God is doing a *new thing*. Therefore, whatever we are expressing will have the newness and freshness of the

Lord on it. This requires that we come out of the old and into the new. One other thing about a *poem* is it has to be read normally in a *rhythm*. Without reading a poem in a rhythm, we don't get the effect of it or even understand it. It is very important in our life that we find our *rhythm*. In *The Message* paraphrase of the Bible, we find the famous Matthew 11:28-30 scripture. This is the portion where Jesus declares that His yoke is easy and His burden is light. Notice how this version expresses it.

> *Are you tired? Worn out? Burned out on religion? Come to me. Get away with me and you'll recover your life. I'll show you how to take a real rest. Walk with me and work with me—watch how I do it. Learn the unforced rhythms of grace. I won't lay anything heavy or ill-fitting on you. Keep company with me and you'll learn to live freely and lightly.*

Wow! We are told in the midst of our oldness to find God's *rhythms of grace.* As we discover the Lord's unforced rhythms of grace, we stop trying to please Him from our own efforts and simply step into His pleasure. We begin to live life from His nature that was imparted to us at the time of our salvation. This is a huge part of us unlocking and stepping into the newness of the Lord. First John 3:9 speaks of this nature that we have received from the Lord.

> *Whoever has been born of God does not sin, for His seed remains in him; and he cannot sin, because he has been born of God.*

The word *seed* in this scripture is the Greek word *sperma*. It means "something sown." It speaks of the *male sperm*. The Lord is declaring that just like a man impregnates a woman through an act of intimacy, so He impregnated us with His seed. The sperm of a man mixed with the egg within a woman will cause a baby to be produced. This child can and will manifest the nature of the father (as well as the mother) as it grows and matures.

Several years ago, I was doing some work on my computer. I had on my reading glasses to help me not to strain to see. As I paused my work for a few seconds, the computer went to sleep and the screen went black. As I looked into the blackened screen to continue my work, I saw my own reflection. For a split second I thought, *How did my dad who died several years ago get into my computer?* This thought occurred to me because for the first time I became aware that I looked very much like my earthly father, especially with my glasses on. I had never considered that I looked that much like him. However, at that moment I saw him in me. By the way, my father was a very handsome man. I was in my 50s when this moment took place. As I said, I had not considered that I looked like Welton Henderson. Yet there he was in my computer. Then it occurred to me that because his seed was in me, the more mature I became in the natural, the more the reflection of my dad manifested.

This is exactly what happens with us as God's seed lives in us. His nature begins to take over our life. As the scripture we cited declares, "We cannot sin." This is because His seed is in us. This doesn't mean it's impossible for us to sin. It means that we cannot sin and be happy in life, because the nature of God in me will not allow it. This is why those who would say that grace allows them to live any way they want are deceived. The real grace of God that imparts to us the nature of the Lord will require holiness and purity of us. Titus 2:11 reveals what the real grace of God is.

For the grace of God that brings salvation has appeared to all men, teaching us that, denying ungodliness and worldly lusts, we should live soberly, righteously, and godly in the present age.

I am concerned that much of the present *grace message* being preached today is a *false grace* message. When it is declared or implies that we can live any way we want, this is dangerous. We are not free to fulfill the lusts and appetites of the flesh and be saved. In fact, if we have received the real grace of God that brings salvation, we will not desire sin. We will abhor it and not want it in our life. This will be a result of the nature of God living in us. This doesn't say we will not be tempted or even sin. However, should this occur, we will not be able to stand it until we repent and have God's cleansing in our life. This is because His nature by His grace is in us! This reality is driving us toward an ever increasing life of holiness and purity. This is a part of coming out of the old and into the new that God has for us. So many people feel stuck in an old place. I have good news. What I have just described can and will be your portion. You will be able to move from the old of sorrow, anguish, and grief into the new of joy, fulfillment, and deep satisfaction.

For me, this happened when I learned how to cancel the devil's legal right to work against me and hold me in an old place. I believe this will happen for you as well. We will learn how to come out of the old and into the new as we function in the Courts of Heaven. If you're like me, you will see the prophetic promises of God become yours. You will no longer wish for them to occur. You will see them in reality.

As I come before Your Courts, Lord, I ask that You might bring me from the old places of despair and disillusionment into the new of fulfilled promises, hopes, and dreams. Let the old fall away, and let the new be seen in my life. I declare before You that I am a new creation in You. Let all things become new in my life. I ask in Jesus' Name, amen.

CHAPTER 2

Revoking the Legal Claim of Words

I am reminded of a dream that I had in the midst of a struggle we were in. In the natural, we had moved back to Waco, Texas, to replant a church that had been there. The reason for this move was because the word of the Lord had come to me. The Lord had said, "Don't give away your and your children's rights to that city." In the natural, I had no desire to go back to Waco. There had been quite a bit of pain we had experienced there through betrayal, loss, and lies. I really did not want anything to do with it. Yet the Lord had clearly spoken.

We did move back. We began a work to replace the one that had been lost. The work began in a modest way. The previous work had actually grown into an apostolic expression. We had quite a few churches planted that had formed a network of churches and ministries. There was a Bible school to train pastors and other ministers to plant other churches. We were on television six days a week in several stations and networks in the world. We had a Christian school that operated at one time. There was a ministry to the poor that touched the city. We owned a 72,000-square-foot building with a 1,500-seat auditorium to facilitate all that we were doing.

Again, at the word of the Lord, we had transitioned out of "pastoring" this work to overseeing it from an "apostolic" standpoint. This meant that I was no longer hands-on on a daily basis, but I was still esteemed and understood to be the apostolic father of the work. The problem was that the person who was set in place to pastor the work under the apostolic structure became unfaithful. He became so filled with selfish ambition that it resulted in the work being destroyed from its original place of power and influence. It was a very sad affair. This unfaithful man's desire to have something for himself caused him to allow my character to be destroyed in the eyes of people who at one time had esteemed me. He was at least a party to people believing lies about me so it would work to his ambitious desires.

I thought that I was done in Waco. The Lord had opened the world for me, and I was being privileged to speak God's word to nations. Then the word concerning not giving away my and my children's rights to the city had come. As we in obedience began to replant a work, it became apparent that something was resisting these efforts. We could only get it so far. It was like a wall was there that we couldn't get through. I then began to get revelation through different means. I realized that four of my former staff members in the work had spoken words against me. These words were being taken by the devil and were being used against me in the Courts of Heaven. I have learned this principle throughout the process of functioning in the Courts of Heaven. If there are words spoken against you, these words become ammunition for the devil's efforts to thwart your kingdom purpose. This is especially true if these words come from certain sources. There are at least three sources that can release words that the devil will take into the Courts of Heaven against us.

The first one is words from people whose authority you are under. This can be parents, husbands, employers, church leaders, and even civil authorities. Anyone whose authority you are connected to can and will be used in a destructive way against you in the Courts of Heaven. Romans 13:1-5 shows the significant place God has given to authority we are to honor.

> *Let every soul be subject to the governing authorities. For there is no authority except from God, and the authorities that exist are appointed by God. Therefore whoever resists the authority resists the ordinance of God, and those who resist will bring judgment on themselves. For rulers are not a terror to good works, but to evil. Do you want to be unafraid of the authority? Do what is good, and you will have praise from the same. For he is God's minister to you for good. But if you do evil, be afraid; for he does not bear the sword in vain; for he is God's minister, an avenger to execute wrath on him who practices evil. Therefore you must be subject, not only because of wrath but also for conscience' sake.*

If authority gives an evil report about you, it can result in a judgment against you from the Courts of Heaven. Hebrews

13:17 implies that if authority gives a less than good report it will work against us.

> *Obey those who rule over you, and be submissive, for they watch out for your souls, as those who must give account. Let them do so with joy and not with grief, for that would be unprofitable for you.*

This scripture says that if authority is grieved by you and their report of you is evil, it can be unprofitable for you. This means, among other things, that the devil uses the report of authority over you to build cases against you in the Courts of Heaven. We must live under authority in a righteous way, but also know how to undo any words from authority against us.

The second dimension of words against us that the devil uses is words of those who carry spiritual authority. You may not be under the authority of these, but because they have gained a place in God, their words can be damaging to us. There is a difference in positional authority and those who have spiritual authority. People can have spiritual authority but not be recognized in the natural with positional authority. It also works the other way. It is possible to have a position of authority but carry no real spiritual authority. Spiritual authority can be seen in what Jesus said about speaking to the mountain in Matthew 17:19-20. Jesus said that if we believe and carry spiritual authority, we can speak and declare, and things that seem immovable will move.

> *Then the disciples came to Jesus privately and said, "Why could we not cast it out?" So Jesus said to them, "Because of your unbelief; for assuredly, I say to you, if you have faith as a mustard seed, you will say to this mountain, 'Move from*

here to there,' and it will move; and nothing will be impossible for you."

In their attempt to remove a demon, they found themselves completely inept. They asked Jesus why this demon couldn't be removed. Jesus' response was that it was an issue of faith. We can see from this that spiritual authority is connected to the faith realm. If we are able to believe, then we will carry authority to remove seemingly immovable things. This is spiritual authority revealed. Whoever carries this spiritual authority allowed by God will be able to undo demonic resistance. This has an effect in the dimensions of the Courts of Heaven. Whoever has been allowed by God to significantly carry authority, if they choose to use that authority destructively, it can have a negative effect. Paul was aware of this. He addressed it in 2 Corinthians 10:8.

> *For even if I should boast somewhat more about our authority, which the Lord gave us for edification and not for your destruction, I shall not be ashamed.*

If someone who carries this authority speaks evil against us, the devil can grab their words. He will take their words against us and declare them before the Courts of Heaven. He can petition the Courts of Heaven and declare, "These whom You have granted authority say this (something evil) about them." People who are apostles, prophets, or one of the other five-fold ministry gifts can fall into this category. I actually had a very high-profile prophet who began to speak against me. When I heard about this, I laughed, knowing I was not guilty of what they were accusing me of. However, then my life began to fall apart. I had to deal with this person's accusations and attacks against me in the Courts of Heaven. The devil was taking their words and building a case against me. The result was serious devastation that began to come into my life, family, and ministry. The devil was claiming a right against me because of the words of this person/prophet. I was not and am not under their authority, but they carry spiritual authority in God. We must know how to undo the words of those in positions of authority and those who carry spiritual authority. Otherwise, a curse can come on our life. The words being spoken grant the curse a legal right to land. This is revealed in Proverbs 26:2.

Like a flitting sparrow, like a flying swallow, so a curse without cause shall not alight.

The words of these who are in authority in either realm will give curses a right to land and light against us. This can bring destructive results. However, we can go into the Courts of Heaven and revoke and annul the rights of these words.

The third realm of words that can have power against us in the Courts of Heaven are words from those we are or have been in covenant with. This applies to the words of my former staff members. In ministry, I never operated from an employer-employee standard. I believed, and still do, that the order for the kingdom of God is covenant. Therefore, when I hired and set in place people to be on my staff, I felt we had entered covenant together. Instead of them being my employees, they were my team. Together, we would advance the kingdom of God. We would function as David and his mighty men did. First Chronicles 12:20-22 shows that great warriors came to David until it was like the army of God.

When he went to Ziklag, those of Manasseh who defected to him were Adnah, Jozabad, Jediael, Michael, Jozabad,

Elihu, and Zillethai, captains of the thousands who were from Manasseh. And they helped David against the bands of raiders, for they were all mighty men of valor, and they were captains in the army. For at that time they came to David day by day to help him, until it was a great army, like the army of God.

David entered covenant with them and they with him. This is a picture of how the kingdom of God is to function. My heart was and is that there would be a team bound together by covenant. This team would have the power and spiritual authority to bring down satanic strongholds. However, because this was how I operated, when these former team members/staff began to speak against me, the devil could use their words. We actually see what happens in 1 Peter 3:7 when those in covenant come to disagreement.

Husbands, likewise, dwell with them with understanding, giving honor to the wife, as to the weaker vessel, and as being heirs together of the grace of life, that your prayers may not be hindered.

Notice that if there is a problem in the covenant relationship, then prayer power is lost. Our prayers that should be dynamic and flow with authority are hindered. This word *hindered* in the Greek is *ekkopto*. It means "to cut down, cut off, chop." When covenant relationships are weakened and even broken, it has a very negative effect on the spiritual authority we carry. This is true in marriage, but also other realms of covenant as well. This is what happened to me with the original team in Waco. When I returned to Waco, the powers of darkness within that region used the words of my former staff as legal right to resist me. I didn't know what to do about this. I honestly did not feel I had anything to repent for concerning these who had broken covenant with me by their words. I didn't feel I was wrong or to be blamed. I knew the devil was making a case against me connected to their words; however, I didn't know how to answer that case or deal with it. Then I had this dream.

In the dream, I found myself in the courts of Waco, Texas. The truth is, I didn't know a place like this existed. I had been asked many times about different courts in the spirit world. I actually had leaned toward the fact that there was just the court revealed and seen in Daniel 7:9-10.

> *I watched till thrones were put in place, and the Ancient of Days was seated; His garment was white as snow, and the hair of His head was like pure wool. His throne was a fiery flame, its wheels a burning fire; a fiery stream issued and came forth from before Him. A thousand thousands ministered to Him; ten thousand times ten thousand stood before Him. The court was seated, and the books were opened.*

This is the purest picture we have of the Courts of Heaven in scripture. Now, however, I am having this dream about a court that is ruling a geographical area. I became aware that there seemed to be courts over regions. This is where principalities that are assigned to regions can make their case against the purposes of God. In other words, they petition the court where they are. They seek to create legal resistance against God's intent and will. I knew that the constraint I was feeling and seeing in the early stages of the new work was because of legal issues against me. These issues were a result of the words spoken by my former team.

As I stood in the court in my dream, I saw two tables before me. They were sitting in this courtroom as you would see them in a natural court. The table on the left had papers lying on it. I knew these papers were cases against me. As I stood looking at these papers/cases, I was perplexed. I didn't know how to answer them. Normally, the answer to a case against us is solved through our repentance. We repent, and then the blood of Jesus is free to speak for us. This is found in 1 John 1:7 and Hebrews 12:24.

> *But if we walk in the light as He is in the light, we have*
> *fellowship with one another, and the blood of Jesus Christ*
> *His Son cleanses us from all sin.*
>
> *To Jesus the Mediator of the new covenant, and to the blood*
> *of sprinkling that speaks better things than that of Abel.*

Walking in the light does not speak of perfect living. Walking in the light speaks of honest living. We are willing to repent and bring out of darkness any of our failures and sins. When we do this, the blood of Jesus is free to cleanse us from all sin. This is because the blood of sprinkling, or Jesus' blood, is speaking and giving testimony from the mercy seat of Heaven. Through our repentance, we gain the advantage of what the blood is saying. The blood of Jesus in the Holiest of Holies in Heaven grants God the legal right to forgive us. Remember that God has always had a desire and longing to forgive us. He didn't have the legal right to do this until Jesus died and gave His blood. Until that transaction, God could only roll sins away for a year, according to Hebrews 10:1-4.

> *For the law, having a shadow of the good things to come,*
> *and not the very image of the things, can never with these*
> *same sacrifices, which they offer continually year by year,*

make those who approach perfect. For then would they not have ceased to be offered? For the worshipers, once purified, would have had no more consciousness of sins. But in those sacrifices there is a reminder of sins every year. For it is not possible that the blood of bulls and goats could take away sins.

We are told that every year when the offerings were made for the sins of the people, they remembered their sins all over. The blood of bulls and goats that was offered could not legally expunge the sin. This is why the offerings were made every year. But when Jesus died and offered His body and blood, this was the perfect offering. He once and for all offered Himself. Hebrews 9:24-28 clearly shows us that the perfect sacrifice of Jesus was all that was needed. This sacrifice is the legal work required to deal with our every sin and bring us to justification.

For Christ has not entered the holy places made with hands, which are copies of the true, but into heaven itself, now to appear in the presence of God for us; not that He should offer Himself often, as the high priest enters the Most Holy Place every year with blood of another—He then would have had to suffer often since the foundation of the world; but now, once at the end of the ages, He has appeared to put away sin by the sacrifice of Himself. And as it is appointed for men to die once, but after this the judgment, so Christ was offered once to bear the sins of many. To those who eagerly wait for Him He will appear a second time, apart from sin, for salvation.

This is why Jesus' blood is the answer to any and all accusations against us. His blood is speaking on our behalf to dismiss every case satan would bring. When we repent and walk in the light as He is in the light, this blood speaks for us. Based on the testimony of His blood, every case against us is dismissed.

I use this principle on a daily basis. I understand the power of His speaking blood. Yet in this situation of my former staff speaking against me, I simply felt no need for repentance. Therefore, I did not know how to answer this case that was on the table against me and the purposes of God in Waco. I was willing to repent if that was what was needed, but I honestly didn't feel I had done anything wrong. I felt, and still do, that those who had been on my staff had rebelled and not abided by the covenant standards we operated in. I had forgiven them, but I simply felt no conviction that I was wrong and should repent.

As I looked at this unanswered case resisting me in the Courts, a young man I did not know stood up. He was about 30 in age with sandy red hair. He spoke in the Courts and said of me, "He has a good spirit." I knew he was giving testimony about me. However, I wasn't impressed with what he said. The thought I immediately had was, "That's all you've got?" Based on his testimony, though, the case against me was immediately dismissed! Instantly, I knew several things. I was aware that the principalities and powers in the Waco, Texas, region could not use the words of my former staff against me any longer. I knew that there might still be words spoken against me. However, these words could not have any power to resist the purposes of God in me and through me. The case the devil had built against me from those who had been in covenant with me was now gone!

The second thing I was aware of was that even though this was now done for me, the breakthrough now gained for me was for my generation. I had this consciousness that breakthrough for my children would have to be gained by them. They would have to deal with any case against themselves in the Courts of Heaven. This is consistent with scripture. For instance, scripture says in Acts 13:36 that David had a generational assignment.

> *For David, after he had served his own generation by the will of God, fell asleep, was buried with his fathers, and saw corruption.*

David very much had a generational heart for his children and the purposes of God. He prepared for the purposes of God to be done through his children. Remember that God would not allow David to build Him a house because he had shed blood. First Chronicles 22:7-10 shows that God appointed Solomon, the son of David, to build His house. David had great passion and longing to build this house, but he was forbidden. The assignment was given instead to the next generation.

> *And David said to Solomon: "My son, as for me, it was in my mind to build a house to the name of the Lord my God; but the word of the Lord came to me, saying, 'You have shed much blood and have made great wars; you shall not build a house for My name, because you have shed much blood on the earth in My sight. Behold, a son shall be born to you, who shall be a man of rest; and I will give him rest from all his enemies all around. His name shall be Solomon, for I will give peace and quietness to Israel in his days. He shall build a house for My name, and he shall be My son, and I will be his Father; and I will establish the throne of his kingdom over Israel forever.'"*

The generation after David had another assignment in the purposes of God. Whereas David had subdued the enemies through war, Solomon would build the house. This is the way of the Lord. Daniel 4:3 clearly declares that the intent of God is from generation to generation.

> *How great are His signs, and how mighty His wonders! His kingdom is an everlasting kingdom, and His dominion is from generation to generation.*

Dominion is the enforcement of the kingdom of God into practical place. In other words, it is when the kingdom rule of God is forcibly set into place and its effects are seen. Notice that this occurs progressively from generation to generation. This is what we are witnessing in David subduing enemies and then Solomon building the house. There are differing assignments from generation to generation so that the dominion of God might be seen on earth.

This is what I knew in the dream. The case against me in Waco, Texas, based on the words of former staff members, was now gone. However, my children would need to deal with their own issues before the Courts of Heaven for greater breakthrough to come in the assignment they carry. I knew I could not do it for them. They had to do it themselves. Even though I have a heart for the purposes of God beyond my own generation, my jurisdiction in the Courts was only for my sphere and time. Remember that the word of God that brought me back to Waco to replant this work was, "Don't give away your and your children's rights in this city." From this dream I had an even greater understanding that I had completed my assignment in the city. The cases against me had been dismissed. The powers of darkness no longer had a right to resist God's will there. My children would not have to deal with the legal rights of the devil against their efforts because of something against me. This was now over! However, they would need to do their own business and transactions in the Courts of Heaven to take the work of God further in this city and region. This is what they are doing today.

One more thing I would highlight is the young man who gave testimony in the Courts of Waco was from the *cloud of witnesses*. Of course, the cloud of witnesses is a heavenly dimension where those who have died and belong to Jesus are in existence. Hebrews 12:1-2 gives us exciting insight into this realm.

> *Therefore we also, since we are surrounded by so great a cloud of witnesses, let us lay aside every weight, and the sin which so easily ensnares us, and let us run with endurance the race that is set before us, looking unto Jesus, the author and finisher of our faith, who for the joy that was set before Him endured the cross, despising the shame, and has sat down at the right hand of the throne of God.*

My purpose here is not to do an exhaustive teaching on the cloud of witnesses. However, they are very much involved in what is happening on earth today. I believe the cloud of witnesses is a part of Jesus' present-day ministry for us and God's will on earth. We know that Jesus is our present-day Intercessor according to Hebrews 7:25. In His resurrected place, He is interceding for us to come into the fullness of God's will.

> *Therefore He is also able to save to the uttermost those who come to God through Him, since He always lives to make intercession for them.*

Save to the uttermost implies that we are coming into everything Jesus died for us to have and accomplish. Jesus didn't just die and legally set into place covenant privileges for us. He is also today interceding and praying for us before the Father. He is reminding the Father of His legal work on our behalf and its power for us. This testimony of Jesus in our stead will bring us into everything meant for us to have and fulfill. It would appear that the cloud of witnesses is a part of this process in the heavenly realm. The word *witness* from Hebrews 12:1 is the Greek word *martus.* This word means "judicially a witness or one who brings a record." It also means "a martyr." This tells us that the cloud of witnesses are those who chose the will of God ahead of their own desires. There are those in Heaven who got there by the blood of Jesus but have no reward. First Corinthians 3:14-15 tells us that some will be in heaven but will have no reward because of the way they spent their lives.

> *If anyone's work which he has built on it endures, he will receive a reward. If anyone's work is burned, he will suffer loss; but he himself will be saved, yet so as through fire.*

Martyrs are not just those who gave their physical lives for the purposes of God to be done on earth. Martyrs are those who chose God's will and desire rather than their own. They laid down their life to do His will. These can be a part of this elite group called the cloud of witnesses. They can function judicially in the Courts of Heaven. If this is true, then they are a part of Jesus' intercessory ministry for us. Hebrews 12:23 shows that these in the cloud of witnesses are joined to Jesus perfectly.

To the general assembly and church of the firstborn who are registered in heaven, to God the Judge of all, to the spirits of just men made perfect.

The cloud of witnesses is referred to here as *the spirit of just men made perfect*. In other words, they are perfectly joined to Jesus. In Heaven, the corruption has put on incorruption and the mortal has put on immortality. First Corinthians 15:53 declares this.

For this corruptible must put on incorruption, and this mortal must put on immortality.

This scripture is speaking of when we get our new, glorified bodies at the return of Jesus. This is when our salvation will be complete. Now, however, those who are in Heaven have perfect spirits and souls. Our bodies will be redeemed. In the present, they are the *spirits of just men made perfect and in perfect union with Jesus.* We are told in 2 Timothy 2:11-12 that we will reign with Him if we have suffered with Him. This is a statement that can mean the heavenly position we will be granted because we chose His desire while here on the earth.

This is a faithful saying: For if we died with Him, we shall also live with Him. If we endure, we shall also reign with Him. If we deny Him, He also will deny us.

Notice that if we take on His death in the sense of dying to ourselves in this life, we shall live with Him. If we take suffering instead of choosing our own way, we will reign with Him. I think this clearly lets us know we get to be a part of His intercessory ministry in Heaven. I've said all of this to let it be known that when the young man stood up on my behalf, he was doing it with the same passion of Jesus. He was allowed to perfectly give testimony on my behalf. His activity from the cloud of witnesses, in perfect union with Jesus, had power before the Courts of Heaven.

The final thing I would address is the testimony given about me. Remember that the young man declared, "He has a good spirit." As said before, I was not impressed with what he was saying about me. Yet it was a sufficient testimony to dismiss the case against me. What I did not realize as I heard this testimony was it struck at the heart of the accusations against me. The accusations against me by my former staff, which the devil built his case against me with, had a common denominator. It all said I was unscrupulous, selfish, dishonest, and even unethical. When it was declared that I had a good spirit, that word from one who was esteemed in Heaven erased and eradicated those accusations. The devil's case against me was dismissed. This allowed me to come out of the old and into the new that God had for me.

Unanswered, the case in the court would have stopped and prohibited me from the next season that God had for me. When this case was dismissed, the new work that had been hindered suddenly began to prosper. We tripled in size and attendance within the next month or so. We were able to get things in place and see prosperity come on many different levels. I was able to hand the work off to my son and his wife in fulfillment of the prophetic word. They are now building from their generation for the times to come. None of this could have happened without the case against me being answered from the cloud of witnesses and in the Courts of Heaven.

Perhaps there is something against you in the Courts of Heaven that is hindering the new that God has for you. The Lord desperately wants to move you into the new season. He wants to unstick you and propel you into the newest places. I want to help you maneuver in the Courts of Heaven to see this occur. First of all, however, we need to see the reality of the Courts of Heaven and how they operate in a greater way. We will pull back the veil on this in the next chapter and take a look.

As I come into Your Presence and before Your Courts, Lord, I ask that all words against me be revoked and annulled. I ask that any whose authority I have been under, any who carry authority with You, and any whom I have been in covenant with, should they have spoken words against me, would You let them be repealed and revoked in Jesus' Name. I repent for any place I am guilty of what they say. I ask for Your precious blood of sprinkling to speak for me. I also forgive them for any and all words they have spoken against me. I ask that it not be laid to their charge. Forgive them, Lord, I ask in Jesus' Name. Thank You, Lord, that I am accepted before You and these words' effects are now removed. Thank You that I am now free to move from the old and into the new. Anything satan has legally used against me is now repealed in Jesus' Name, amen!

CHAPTER 3

The Unseen Realm of the Court of Heaven

Getting unstuck, escaping delay, and coming into the promises of God requires operation in the Courts of Heaven. At least it did for me. It seems that I experienced delay for a good two decades. I was very frustrated and had even become a skeptic. Not seeing the prophetic promises of God happen caused anger, bitterness, and unbelief to develop in my heart. I am not justifying this. This was just the true fact of things. Then I discovered the Courts of Heaven and its reality.

I would point out that the Courts of Heaven is a spiritual dimension. What I mean by this is it is a real place in the unseen world. We as Christian believers understand that the unseen world influences the natural realm we live in. If we want to change things in this natural world, then things must shift in the unseen world first. Second Corinthians 4:17-18 makes a statement about the unseen world.

*For our light affliction, which is but for a moment, is work-
ing for us a far more exceeding and eternal weight of glory,
while we do not look at the things which are seen, but at the
things which are not seen. For the things which are seen are
temporary, but the things which are not seen are eternal.*

The apostle Paul declares strength for getting through trials,
testing, and difficult times is found in a belief in the unseen realm.
He declares that this natural world is temporary but that which
is unseen in eternal. Any suffering we go through in this present
world will result in a higher realm of function and glory in the spiritual dimension. Of course, Jesus alluded to this unseen world. In
John 3:13, Jesus spoke of His function and life in this unseen realm
while He lived a natural life on earth. In other words, He spoke of
living in two worlds at one time—the seen and the unseen.

*No one has ascended to heaven but He who came down
from heaven, that is, the Son of Man who is in heaven.*

Jesus, speaking of Himself as the Son of Man, said He came
down from heaven, ascended to heaven, and even as He spoke was
in heaven. In referring to *heaven*, Jesus was speaking of the *heavenly realm* or the unseen dimension. This statement can be seen as
declaring that Jesus had learned to live in a heavenly realm while
alive on earth. This is why Jesus spoke of *seeing* what the Father was
doing in John 5:19-20. He proclaimed that this was the key to the
miracles He did.

*Then Jesus answered and said to them, "Most assuredly, I
say to you, the Son can do nothing of Himself, but what
He sees the Father do; for whatever He does, the Son also
does in like manner. For the Father loves the Son, and shows*

*Him all things that He Himself does; and He will show
Him greater works than these, that you may marvel."*

Jesus was in such union with the Father that He saw into the spiritual dimension and mimicked what He saw there. The result was the supernatural demonstration of heaven revealed on earth. We too should desire to operate in the unseen world by faith. In fact, this is what faith is. Faith is believing in and operating in the unseen realm according to Hebrews 11:1.

*Now faith is the substance of things hoped for, the evidence
of things not seen.*

Notice faith is the evidence of what we can't see. When we look through Hebrews 11, we see this echoed over and over. Hebrews 11:3 shows us the worlds were *not* created out of nothing. They were created by what was in the unseen world.

*By faith we understand that the worlds were framed by
the word of God, so that the things which are seen were not
made of things which are visible.*

In Christian circles, it is commonly taught that God made the world from nothing. This is not true. The worlds were fashioned by things not visible yet very real! The spoken word of God unleashed that which was invisible to create the visible. This is still how things work. We must realize how to unlock the unseen world to fashion the world we desire today! Hebrews 11:27 tells us that Moses endured and functioned by seeing into the unseen realm.

*By faith he forsook Egypt, not fearing the wrath of the king;
for he endured as seeing Him who is invisible.*

Faith is functioning in the unseen realm. This is what empowered Moses to do what he did. He learned to come into agreement with the heavenly realm. The result was a nation delivered from Egypt. He discovered how to live in this dimension while living a natural life on earth. This is what we are called to as well. The Court of Heaven is a spiritual dimension we step into by faith. This is why it is declared in Daniel 7:9-10 that Daniel *watched*.

> *I watched till thrones were put in place, and the Ancient of Days was seated; His garment was white as snow, and the hair of His head was like pure wool. His throne was a fiery flame, its wheels a burning fire; a fiery stream issued And came forth from before Him. A thousand thousands ministered to Him; ten thousand times ten thousand stood before Him. The court was seated, and the books were opened.*

Daniel as a *seer* watched as the Court of Heaven was set into place and began to operate. He was seeing into the unseen realm. If we are to function in the Courts of Heaven, we must move in faith. The Court of Heaven isn't a new method of praying; it is a dimension of the spirit realm. If we can understand this and simply operate in faith, we can see huge breakthrough ensue.

Jesus actually grants us insight into operating in this unseen realm of the Courts in Luke 18:1-8. He unveils some principles that can empower us to move in this dimension.

> *Then He spoke a parable to them, that men always ought to pray and not lose heart, saying: "There was in a certain city a judge who did not fear God nor regard man. Now there was a widow in that city; and she came to him, saying, 'Get justice for me from my adversary.' And he would not for a while; but afterward he said within himself, 'Though I do not fear God nor regard man, yet because this widow*

*troubles me I will avenge her, lest by her continual coming
she weary me.'"*

*Then the Lord said, "Hear what the unjust judge said. And
shall God not avenge His own elect who cry out day and
night to Him, though He bears long with them? I tell you
that He will avenge them speedily. Nevertheless, when the
Son of Man comes, will He really find faith on the earth?"*

Jesus places prayer in a judicial setting in this story. He is seeking
to empower us to get answers to previously unanswered prayer. This
is why it is said that the purpose of this teaching was so the disciples
wouldn't become weary and quit praying. The only reason people
quit praying is because it doesn't seem to be working. The temptation
to stop praying is because there seem to be no results. Jesus is not just
encouraging His disciples to keep praying through this parable; He is
telling them "why" they should keep praying. He is unveiling through
this teaching an awareness of what is happening in the unseen world.

There are five principles for functioning in the spiritual dimension of the Courts of Heaven revealed in Jesus' story. First of all, we
see we have an *adversary*. The word *adversary* in these verses is the
Greek word *antidikos*. This word means "one who brings a lawsuit."
We see it used many places in scripture. One of the most powerful
places it is used is in 1 Peter 5:8. We can see clearly who our *adversary* is from this scripture.

*Be sober, be vigilant; because your adversary the devil walks
about like a roaring lion, seeking whom he may devour.*

The devil and his forces, or our *adversary*, is the one bringing
a lawsuit against us. His power to devour us is found in his legal
action against us. Satan cannot devour or consume us unless he

discovers and makes a case against us from a legal perspective. The widow in the story is being harassed and devoured because of her adversary's activities. One of the clearest places we see this happening is in the story of Job. An accusation is leveled against Job by satan in Job 1:6-12. This is a judicial setting in the unseen realm. As a result of satan bringing this case against Job, Job was thrown into unbelievable trouble and tribulation.

> *Now there was a day when the sons of God came to present themselves before the Lord, and Satan also came among them. And the Lord said to Satan, "From where do you come?"*
>
> *So Satan answered the Lord and said, "From going to and fro on the earth, and from walking back and forth on it."*
>
> *Then the Lord said to Satan, "Have you considered My servant Job, that there is none like him on the earth, a blameless and upright man, one who fears God and shuns evil?"*
>
> *So Satan answered the Lord and said, "Does Job fear God for nothing? Have You not made a hedge around him, around his household, and around all that he has on every side? You have blessed the work of his hands, and his possessions have increased in the land. But now, stretch out Your hand and touch all that he has, and he will surely curse You to Your face!"*
>
> *And the Lord said to Satan, "Behold, all that he has is in your power; only do not lay a hand on his person."*
>
> *So Satan went out from the presence of the Lord.*

Notice that God asked satan where he had been. His answer was, "Going to and from on the earth, and walking back and forth on it." This is consistent with what the Bible declares in other places. As we saw in 1 Peter 5:8, the devil is *walking about*. This means he is searching for any legal reason he can find to bring a case against the people of God.

This is what happened to me and I didn't know it. Just like I'm sure Job was at a loss to explain *why* his life suddenly was brought to destruction. I'm sure initially he had no awareness of what had transpired in the unseen world that was allowing this. He would later at least have an idea of what was happening. He would long to approach God in His throne and answer for himself in the Courts of Heaven. He would realize that the answer to his dilemma was to make his case in the Courts of Heaven. This too is our solution. If we can make our case before the Courts of Heaven, we can see victory and the removing of the old and the moving into the new seasons of life!

As I stand in Your Courts, Lord, I decree I believe in their existence. I desire to operate in this unseen world of Your judicial place. I declare that You, Lord, are the Judge of all. I desire to be freed by this Court to move out of the old and into the new that You have for me. Free me from every stress and distress. Move me into the fullness of what You have promised, in Jesus' Name, amen.

CHAPTER 4

The Court of Heaven Revealed

Mary and I had been living a blessed life. Sure, we had challenges and struggles from time to time, but mostly we were happy and strong. Then, everything changed. Much like Job, we found ourselves in trouble and devastation. My theology at that time made me think surely there was something wrong with me that was allowing this. I had no awareness of the legal realms of the spirit world. I didn't know that the devil could be making a case against me that was causing the devouring that was happening in our life on many levels. I now know that I had become a greater threat and therefore the devil searched out a legal right against me. Satan had commissioned a search to be made to see what there was in my family history that would grant him a legal claim against me.

The devil cannot just devour because he wants to. He must discover a legal right to do it from. The legal right he discovered against me initially was a covenant made with demons in my ancestry. When this was found in my history, it gave him the legal right to devour and destroy me. Just like with Job, he made a case against me in the Courts of Heaven. Only through prophetic input did I come to the realization of this covenant with demons from my bloodline. Little did I know that this covenant with demons was giving the devil the legal right to presently devour, but was also the culprit causing the delay in my life. The delay and being stuck for two decades had its roots in this covenant with demons.

If we are to fully understand this, we must recognize that satan will search out and use what is in our ancestry. This is why the scriptures exhort us to repent for the sins of our *fathers*. Some would consider this not theologically correct from a New Testament standard. However, this mindset can allow the devil the opportunity to bring destruction into our lives. I have watched people deny that anything from their bloodline could have such power. They claim that when Jesus died on the cross all this was eradicated and dealt with. They claim this the whole time their lives, families, finances, and destinies are being destroyed.

Let me be very clear! I believe that Jesus' work on the cross was absolutely legally sufficient to answer any and all cases against us. However, it must be set in place for us if it is to have its desired and intended effect. This is what we are doing when we operate in the Courts of Heaven. Jesus' work on the cross was *all* legal. Everything He did by suffering and dying on the cross was meeting the legal demands for full redemption of us and God's creation. This is why Jesus declared in John 19:30 that it was *finished*.

So when Jesus had received the sour wine, He said, "It is finished!" And bowing His head, He gave up His spirit.

This declaration proclaimed that every legal issue was now met. All the offerings made for all the millennia that had prophesied of what Jesus would do were now fulfilled. Anything and everything legally necessary for the redemption of humanity and creation was accomplished! Now we can take His legal work and present it as evidence in the Courts when asking for decisions from those Courts. For instance, we can cite Isaiah 53:4 when asking the Courts for healing.

> *Surely He has borne our griefs and carried our sorrows; yet we esteemed Him stricken, smitten by God, and afflicted.*

We can remind the Courts that when Jesus died on the cross, He *bore our sicknesses and carried away our pains.* This is the better translation of this scripture because *griefs* refers to sickness while *sorrows* implies pain. This was the legal work of Jesus on the cross for us. The Holy Spirit takes the legal work of Jesus and, on the basis of it, sets in place functionally. This is what John 16:8-11 tells us.

> *And when He has come, He will convict the world of sin, and of righteousness, and of judgment: of sin, because they do not believe in Me; of righteousness, because I go to My Father and you see Me no more; of judgment, because the ruler of this world is judged.*

Jesus is revealing three things the Holy Spirit would convince us about when He was to come. He would convince us of our unbelief. This means the Holy Spirit would war with our unbelief attached to our humanity. He would make us a bold people to believe Him. He would convince us of righteousness and show us His standards for our lives. He would keep us out of legalism and lawlessness. He would cause us to walk righteously before Him.

This third area is the one I want to zero in on. The Holy Spirit would convince us of the judgment that Jesus rendered against the power of darkness when He died on the cross. The legal work of Jesus on the cross caused satan to be judged. However, this judgment has to set into place. This is what the Holy Spirit does. He empowers us to take the legal work of Jesus against the powers of darkness and set them into operation. If we don't know how to do this, we get no benefit from what Jesus has legally done. This is what we do in and from the Courts of Heaven. We take the legal work of Jesus, present it as evidence in the Courts of Heaven, and ask for righteous judgments on the powers of darkness. When this is done, we can get the full effect of all Jesus accomplished on the cross. This cannot happen without the person of the Spirit empowering us to do so. Jesus' legal work can only be executed into place through the Holy Spirit and His activity in us.

Another issue we should look at is the *timing* of the removal of curses and their effect. Galatians 3:13 tells us that the curses from the law were revoked when Jesus died on the cross.

> *Christ has redeemed us from the curse of the law, having become a curse for us (for it is written, "Cursed is everyone who hangs on a tree").*

Jesus' legal work on the cross annulled the power of curses legally. However, just like any other legal work done, it has to be set into place. In fact, the revelations of the apostle Paul and other writers of the New Testament concerning Jesus' activities on the cross are *stated verdicts of the cross.* They are all a declaration of what Jesus legally did. However, they must be set into place or they have no power! The redemption from curses is included in this. Curses have been legally annulled. However, they will not be totally removed until the millennial reign of Jesus. Revelation 22:1-3 unveils this.

> *And he showed me a pure river of water of life, clear as crystal, proceeding from the throne of God and of the Lamb. In the middle of its street, and on either side of the river, was the tree of life, which bore twelve fruits, each tree yielding its fruit every month. The leaves of the tree were for the healing of the nations. And there shall be no more curse, but the throne of God and of the Lamb shall be in it, and His servants shall serve Him.*

Notice that as this full authority of the kingdom is manifest, *there shall be no more curse.* This is when the full effect of all that Jesus did on the cross will be known. To be clear about what I am saying, Galatians 3:13 is the stated verdict of the cross. Revelation 22:1-3 is the full execution of that verdict into place. Until this time, through the power, revelation, and operation of the Holy Spirit we must execute into place Jesus' legal work. One of the ways we do this is by presenting Jesus' work on the cross as legal evidence in the Courts of Heaven. We can then get the full effect of all that Jesus did for us operating in our life.

There is one more scripture connected to this whole issue of understanding how the legal realm of the spirit operates. Ezekiel 18:1-4 is used by those who want to argue against the need to operate in the Courts of Heaven. They will cite this scripture to annul the need to do anything legal.

> *The word of the Lord came to me again, saying, "What do you mean when you use this proverb concerning the land of Israel, saying:*
>
> *"'The fathers have eaten sour grapes, And the children's teeth are set on edge'?*
>
> *"As I live," says the Lord God, "you shall no longer use this proverb in Israel.*
>
> *"Behold, all souls are Mine; The soul of the father As well as the soul of the son is Mine; The soul who sins shall die."*

Those who argue will say that even the Old Testament says that the father's sins cannot be used against us. This is in fact what is being said here. It is the declaration that the sinful activity of the fathers will not have negative repercussions against us. Yet we are clearly told in other parts of the scripture that there is a need to repent for the father's sins or ancestral transgressions. Let me give some scriptures. Exodus 20:4-5 tells us the effect of sin in the bloodline.

> *You shall not make for yourself a carved image—any likeness of anything that is in heaven above, or that is on earth beneath, or that is in the water under the earth; you shall not bow down to them nor serve them. For I, the Lord your God, am a jealous God, visiting the iniquity of the fathers upon the children to the third and fourth generations of those who hate Me.*

When the scripture says that God will visit with iniquity, it is declaring that He will allow satan the right to destroy with it. God Himself is incapable of doing harm and bringing destruction. James 1:17 lets us know that God only does good.

Every good gift and every perfect gift is from above, and comes down from the Father of lights, with whom there is no variation or shadow of turning.

This scripture seems to imply that God is a good God and only does good. However the devil will take the standard of God's word and use it against us in the Court of Heaven. He claims the legal right to bring destruction into our lives and families based on scriptural principles. If our forefathers/mothers committed sin (which they did), the devil's ploy is to use it to harass and destroy our future and destiny. We have to know how to take what Jesus did for us and use it in the Courts of Heaven to silence the rights he is claiming against us.

Another scripture dealing with our forefathers' sin is Leviticus 26:38-42. This scripture shows that is we repent for ourselves and our father's sin we can be brought out of captivity.

You shall perish among the nations, and the land of your enemies shall eat you up. And those of you who are left shall waste away in their iniquity in your enemies' lands; also in their fathers' iniquities, which are with them, they shall waste away.

But if they confess their iniquity and the iniquity of their fathers, with their unfaithfulness in which they were unfaithful to Me, and that they also have walked contrary to Me, and that I also have walked contrary to them and have brought them into the land of their enemies; if their uncircumcised hearts are humbled, and they accept their guilt—then I will remember My covenant with Jacob, and

My covenant with Isaac and My covenant with Abraham
I will remember; I will remember the land.

Notice that we are warned that if we don't deal with our sin and the iniquity of our fathers, it can be used to cause us to *waste away*. This means that there will be a progressive captivity that will bring destruction to our lives. There will be a constant failing that will result in complete devastation. This is because the devil claims a legal right to use the iniquity of our fathers against us.

We also see Daniel repenting not just for his sins but the iniquity of the fathers as well. Daniel 9:16 sees him repenting for the fathers' iniquity that caused them to be brought into captivity. He understands that unless this iniquity it legally dealt with through repentance, they cannot come out of captivity.

O Lord, according to all Your righteousness, I pray, let
Your anger and Your fury be turned away from Your city
Jerusalem, Your holy mountain; because for our sins, and
for the iniquities of our fathers, Jerusalem and Your people
are a reproach to all those around us.

In representing the culture and nation of Israel before the Lord, Daniel repents on their behalf. This includes repentance for the fathers' sin. If this is clear, then why would Ezekiel have prophesied about the sins of the fathers not affecting the children? He did so because this was the prophetic intent of God. God's intention is that the fathers' sins not determine the future and destiny of the children. However, this can only happen *if* there is repentance. When we finish the chapter of Ezekiel 18, we find God giving the stipulation to what He has promised. This can only happen when there is repentance. We see this at the end of Ezekiel 18. In Ezekiel

18:30, God urges the people to repent *so that what He has promised in the previous verses can be theirs!*

> *Therefore I will judge you, O house of Israel, every one according to his ways," says the Lord God. "Repent, and turn from all your transgressions, so that iniquity will not be your ruin.*

Notice that if they don't repent and deal with the *iniquity*, it will be their ruin. Simply put, *iniquity* is the sin of our ancestry. It will destroy futures and destiny. God's intent is that the iniquity of our bloodline cannot be used against us. However, we must repent and allow the blood of Jesus to speak for us to get this benefit. When this occurs, the legal claims against us are removed. Any rights satan is using to withstand us coming out of the old and into the new are revoked. These are some essential understandings to dealing with the adversary that would build cases against us in the Courts of Heaven.

Another one of the five principles we find in Luke 18 about functioning in the Courts of Heaven is this realm is for the *"elect or chosen."* Jesus declared in these verses that if this widow could get a verdict for herself, *how much more would God avenge His elect!* I have met people who actually told me they didn't want to go before the Courts of Heaven. They feared approaching God as judge. However, the Court of Heaven is a place that operates in favor for the chosen of God. It is the place where we as the chosen/elect of God take satan to Court. This is what the widow did to her adversary. The result was a verdict against the adversary that revoked his rights to afflict, harass, and steal from her. She was vindicated as the chosen/elect of God. Ephesians 1:3-4 lets us know this place of choosing we have in God.

> *Blessed be the God and Father of our Lord Jesus Christ, who has blessed us with every spiritual blessing in the heavenly places in Christ, just as He chose us in Him before the foundation of the world, that we should be holy and without blame before Him in love.*

We were chosen in Him before the foundation of the earth. Therefore, we are seen as holy, blameless, and loved by Him. We are blessed with every spiritual blessing. We should understand and believe the position we have been given and boldly approach the Courts of Heaven and make our case. This Court is for us.

Another principle we can learn from Luke 18 about the Courts of Heaven is we can obtain a status there. As Jesus speaks about this widow being able to get a verdict, He speaks of those who *cry out day and night to God.* This is referring to those who have taken the time and effort to build a prayer life. In other words, they have a history with God. This is the one element that so often is missing with those who don't get the desired results from the Courts of Heaven. They have taken the principles and tried to use them as a formula. However, those who have spent the time and discipline to develop this prayer place have a status in the Courts before the Lord. This is not saying that those who haven't done this cannot see breakthrough. It is just saying that those with this history usually get greater results quicker. Hebrews 11:39 gives us insight into those who have a status before the Lord.

And all these, having obtained a good testimony through faith, did not receive the promise.

Those who walked in faith and have sought the Lord as a result have a good testimony. This means they are thought highly of in the heavenly realm. The result is that when they come before the Courts, they are esteemed and regarded. Their request and petition is responded to readily.

When I first went before the Courts of Heaven, the results were very quick. Then I began to try and help others get the same results. Some did. Others did not. I asked those who understood the Courts better than me at that time why this was the case. Their response surprised me. They said I got quick and great results, "Because I had done the work." They were saying that because I had spent years praying, repenting, and seeking the face of God, I had a status before the Courts of Heaven. Therefore, when I intentionally stepped into this realm, my acceptance there was immediate. The breakthrough came quickly. This was a result of having sought Him *day and night.* It is never too late to begin to develop this *status* before the Lord. However, in the absence of this kind of history, we need to just move in faith and cry from our hearts. The Lord will move and render verdicts if we sincerely approach Him.

A fourth thing we can learn from Luke 18 about the Courts of Heaven is that results can be speedy. We are told in these verses that *God will avenge us speedily.* This is what happened to me and really got my attention about the Courts of Heaven. Prayers that I had been praying for years, which seemed like they would not be answered, were answered immediately. When the legal claim of the adversary against me was annulled, God was free to answer my prayers. It wasn't God I was trying to convince to answer me. It was the legal rights of the devil against me that needed to be silenced. When this happened, I came out of the old and into the new. Delay ended, and a new season of life started!

This is what David experienced in 2 Samuel 21:1. There was a famine in the land because Saul, David's predecessor, had broken the covenant that Joshua had made with the Gibeonites. The devil was using this as a legal reason to stop rain and bring famine in the land.

Now there was a famine in the days of David for three years, year after year; and David inquired of the Lord. And the Lord answered, "It is because of Saul and his bloodthirsty house, because he killed the Gibeonites."

Clearly there was prayer being made for the land and for rain. Yet for three years, there was no rain that would allow the land to prosper. Under the direction and insight of the Lord, David reinstituted the covenant with the Gibeonites. Notice what 2 Samuel 21:14 declares.

They buried the bones of Saul and Jonathan his son in the country of Benjamin in Zelah, in the tomb of Kish his father. So they performed all that the king commanded. And after that God heeded the prayer for the land.

God heeded the prayer for the land! David reinstated the covenant with the Gibeonites and took care of the unfinished business of honoring Saul and Jonathan. These two acts removed any and all legal claims that had stopped the Lord from responding to the prayers. It wasn't a matter of convincing God to answer. It was a matter of dealing with legal issues the devil was using to shut up the heavens. When this was removed, the rain from heaven could fall again. We should approach unanswered prayer from a legal perspective. What is the legal reason why God is not answering? If this can be discerned, the answers can come.

The last thing I will mention about secrets and principles to operating in the Courts of Heaven from Luke 18 is that we must do it by faith. The last statement Jesus makes concerning functioning in the judicial system of heaven is *will the Lord really find faith on the earth when He comes.* Among other things, this means that God will be very faithful to this principle; therefore, it should propel people to believe God. It also is declaring that the way we operate in the Courts of Heaven is through faith. Just like with all other realms of the spirit, we enter and function there through faith in Jesus and His blood. This is what grants us access. Hebrews 10:19 is very clear.

> *Therefore, brethren, having boldness to enter the Holiest by the blood of Jesus.*

Jesus' blood has given us access into this spiritual dimension. I don't care who you are, you enter these realms through the blood of Jesus! You do not have to have special anything. All you need is a faith and confidence in God. We come before Him with a true and sincere heart and we are received. Hebrews 10:22 tells us the requirements to approach God in any dimension of the spirit.

> *Let us draw near with a true heart in full assurance of faith, having our hearts sprinkled from an evil conscience and our bodies washed with pure water.*

Our heart must be pure. We must approach in faith through what Jesus has done for us. We must have defilements removed that would speak against us and annihilate faith. We should be water baptized, which repositions us in the spirit world. These four things are what we are told from this scripture in regard to approaching God. We have full access to the presence of God and the Courts of Heaven.

With this said, we do all this through faith. There are some groups who quite frankly get really strange. They would tell you that you need to *see* in the spirit world and operate on a very high prophetic level to do this. This is *not true!* I do not have the prophetic abilities they say are necessary to operate in the Courts of Heaven. However, I do have a history and place in God. I simply come before the Lord with a true heart in faith. I use the limited prophetic senses I have and maneuver in the Courts of Heaven. The result has been massive breakthrough. Quite honestly, I get *more* breakthrough than those who claim all these phenomenal encounters in the spirit world.

You can too. Take God at His word. Move in faith in the principles revealed concerning the Courts of Heaven. Use the prophetic abilities you do have. You will see great breakthrough come. You will step out of the old and into the new that God has for you. You will no longer be restricted by that which has been. You will unlock the next places God has for you and see the covenant promises of God become yours.

Thank You, Lord, that I am granted access into Your Courts because of the blood of Jesus. I thank You that every legal issue from my life or my bloodline is cleansed and washed away. Thank You that the devil loses all legal claims against me. As I stand before Your Courts, by faith I receive all that You did for me on the cross. I humbly repent. I ask, Holy Spirit, that You would take all that Jesus has legally done and apply it in my life. Let all of the devil's legal claims against me be revoked. Move me from the old and into the new, I ask in Jesus' Name, amen.

CHAPTER 5

Resetting Time

One of the main things the devil does to keep us stuck in the old is use up our years. What I mean by this is years pass by and we stay contained in a life God didn't mean for us. We end up living out a limited version of what was purposed for us. The truth is that we are all mortal. We only have so many years allotted to us in this life. We will all die, and those who know Jesus will transition into the heavenly realm. Those who don't will be lost and experience eternal torment. The devil's intent is to seek to cause us to waste the number of our years in delay. We are told in Daniel 7:25 that the anti-Christ spirit intends to do this.

> *He shall speak pompous words against the Most High, shall persecute the saints of the Most High, and shall intend to change times and law. Then the saints shall be given into his hand for a time and times and half a time.*

Intend to change times and law can speak of several different things. One thing that it can mean is that satan wants to interrupt and disrupt the timing of God. If he can do this, he can produce a hope deferred in the saints of God that incapacitates us. When we have our heart set on something God has said and it doesn't happen, this births disappointment. If this occurs enough, it will eradicate real faith. We at best just become faithless Christians who no longer have a heart to believe God. We see this in scripture in several places. The Shunammite woman in the days of Elisha was in this place. She clearly loved God, yet her disappointment in not having a child had placed in her a faithlessness. What I mean by this is there was a place in her heart where it was too painful to believe again. This is the purpose of the devil in interfering with the timing of God.

Before I go into some examples of the devil doing this, let me address the *why*. The ultimate reason why satan would seek to disrupt the timing of God, if not completely stop what is intended, is to stay out of the judgment he is sentenced to. It is clear that ultimately satan will be thrown into the lake of fire and brimstone. Revelation 20:10 shows the devil and all aligned with him being thrown into this place of eternal torment and punishment.

The devil, who deceived them, was cast into the lake of fire and brimstone where the beast and the false prophet are. And they will be tormented day and night forever and ever.

He knows this is his ultimate destination. He understands it. Revelation 12:12 says that satan is aware that his time is short. He recognizes that his ultimate judgment is on the horizon.

Therefore rejoice, O heavens, and you who dwell in them! Woe to the inhabitants of the earth and the sea! For the devil has come down to you, having great wrath, because he knows that he has a short time.

He is seeking to cause as much havoc as possible before the fulfillment of his sentence. He also knows that if he can disrupt the purposes of God on earth, he can extend his freedom. He understands things the people of God do not understand. The time of the culmination of things is not a set date on the calendar. The climax of history and the judgment of satan is tied to the church fulfilling the purposes of God. Peter alludes to this in 2 Peter 3:10-12. He shows that the Day of the Lord, or the return of Jesus and the culmination of history, is connected to the fulfillment of God's purposes. This is joined to the church and its faithful operation.

> *But the day of the Lord will come as a thief in the night, in which the heavens will pass away with a great noise, and the elements will melt with fervent heat; both the earth and the works that are in it will be burned up. Therefore, since all these things will be dissolved, what manner of persons ought you to be in holy conduct and godliness, looking for and hastening the coming of the day of God, because of which the heavens will be dissolved, being on fire, and the elements will melt with fervent heat?*

We are to be *hastening* the culmination of the ages. This word *hastening* in the Greek is *speudo*. It means "to speed." In other words, we are to be speeding up the fulfillment of the prophetic intent of God. The activities of the church can either speed up the purposes of God or can slow them down. Satan knows that if he can disrupt the church from fulfilling the purposes of God, he can extend his stay out of the lake of fire and brimstone. He also knows that the purposes of God that must be fulfilled are tied to God's people fulfilling their call and moving into their destiny. Therefore, he will do everything in his power to disrupt the timing of God. We can see this throughout scripture.

One of the main places we see this is the children of Israel's journey to the Promised Land. A journey that could have taken as little as 11 days took well over 40 years. The disobedience of the children of Israel lengthened the process. Satan was involved in this. He created faithlessness, stubbornness, and unbelief in the hearts of the people. This caused God to sentence them to 40 years of wandering. He waited for a whole generation to die out. He then raised up their children. We see this in Numbers 14:29-31.

> *The carcasses of you who have complained against Me shall fall in this wilderness, all of you who were numbered, according to your entire number, from twenty years old and above. Except for Caleb the son of Jephunneh and Joshua the son of Nun, you shall by no means enter the land which I swore I would make you dwell in. But your little ones, whom you said would be victims, I will bring in, and they shall know the land which you have despised.*

God's purposes were delayed by 40 years because of the disobedience and complaining of His people. We must be very careful not to get into agreement with satan and his forces. This can cause us to forfeit what God has for us. In regard to this, we see in 1 Corinthians 10:5-12 people losing their destinies. These scriptures are expressly about the Israelites and their journeys in the wilderness. They illustrate their rebellion against God and the resulting consequences.

> *But with most of them God was not well pleased, for their bodies were scattered in the wilderness.*

Now these things became our examples, to the intent that we should not lust after evil things as they also lusted. And do not become idolaters as were some of them. As it is written, "The people sat down to eat and drink, and rose up to play." Nor let us commit sexual immorality, as some of them did, and in one day twenty-three thousand fell; nor let us tempt Christ, as some of them also tempted, and were destroyed by serpents; nor complain, as some of them also complained, and were destroyed by the destroyer. Now all these things happened to them as examples, and they were written for our admonition, upon whom the ends of the ages have come.

Therefore let him who thinks he stands take heed lest he fall.

These things happened to them as an example for us to learn from. An entire generation lost its purpose and destiny. It also was party to the disruption of the timing of God. This caused God to have to wait an entire generation before His will could be done—all because a people would not move into faith to inherit the promises of God.

Another place we see the purposes of God delayed is in the children of Israel coming out of Egyptian bondage. In Genesis 15:13, God told Abraham that his descendants would be in bondage for 400 years.

Then He said to Abram: "Know certainly that your descendants will be strangers in a land that is not theirs, and will serve them, and they will afflict them four hundred years."

Yet when the people come out of Egypt, it was in the 430th year of their captivity. Exodus 12:41 gives us the exact number of years they were in the bondage of Egypt.

And it came to pass at the end of the four hundred and thirty years—on that very same day—it came to pass that all the armies of the Lord went out from the land of Egypt.

They were in captivity to Egypt 30 years longer than God said they would be. The time was lengthened and disrupted. God had to wait longer than what was previously intended. Somehow satan was able to interfere with the timing and desire of the Lord. Perhaps the delay of Israel coming out of Egypt by the 400-year mark had to do with Moses killing the Egyptian. Remember, in Exodus 2:11-12 we are told of Moses defending one of his Israelite brothers.

Now it came to pass in those days, when Moses was grown, that he went out to his brethren and looked at their burdens. And he saw an Egyptian beating a Hebrew, one of his brethren. So he looked this way and that way, and when he saw no one, he killed the Egyptian and hid him in the sand.

In Acts 7:22-30, as he is making his declaration, Stephen gives more insight into this occurrence.

And Moses was learned in all the wisdom of the Egyptians, and was mighty in words and deeds.

Now when he was forty years old, it came into his heart to visit his brethren, the children of Israel. And seeing one of them suffer wrong, he defended and avenged him who was oppressed, and struck down the Egyptian. For he supposed that his brethren would have understood that God would deliver them by his hand, but they did not understand. And the next day he appeared to two of them as they were fighting, and tried to reconcile them, saying, "Men, you are brethren; why do you wrong one another?" But he who did his neighbor wrong pushed him away, saying, "Who made you a ruler and a judge over us? Do you want to kill me as you did the Egyptian yesterday?" Then, at this saying, Moses fled and became a dweller in the land of Midian, where he had two sons.

And when forty years had passed, an Angel of the Lord appeared to him in a flame of fire in a bush, in the wilderness of Mount Sinai.

Could it be that the killing of the Egyptian, in Moses' attempt to deliver Israel in own power, actually slowed down the intent of God? Perhaps, if Moses had not taken matters into his own hands, God would have delivered Israel within the next 10 years. This would have placed them right within the timing of God. However, because of Moses' zeal he jumped the gun, so to speak, and ended up in the wilderness for 40 years. This would have meant that Moses' own fleshly efforts got in the way of the timing of God. Moses, as the deliverer, lengthened by 30 years what should have happened in the next 10 years. When Moses should have been delivering Israel from Egyptian bondage, he was hiding in the wilderness because of his erroneous efforts out of his own strength.

How often we do this as well. We have an awareness of what we are called to do, but try to accomplish it in our own strength. We must repent of these efforts. Jesus told us in John 15:5 that we are incapable outside His strength and might.

I am the vine, you are the branches. He who abides in Me, and I in him, bears much fruit; for without Me you can do nothing.

We must learn that any call we have in God must be done in His power, might, and anointing.

Many years ago, as I was preparing for ministry, I had a dream that radically affected and directed my life. I was a young man, desiring to be used of God and to "start" my ministry. In this dream, I was walking up a mountain road with heavy machinery and equipment building the road before me. I remember how slow the equipment and process was moving. I wanted to move faster. As I walked behind the road being built before me, I looked to the left and thought there was enough room to squeeze by and get ahead of the machinery. As I tried to slip around the equipment and move ahead, my foot slipped and I went off the side of the mountain. I found myself hanging off a cliff by my armpits.

I suddenly realized in that moment that my son Adam was on my back. Even though I was in this precarious position, I knew I could hang on. However, I was deeply concerned that Adam might lose his grip and slip and fall. I looked up and saw a man with a pickaxe working on the road. I called to him and urged him to get Adam off my back and to safety. Instead, with supernatural strength, he reached with one hand, grabbed my arm, and picked me up. I knew he was an angel or some other heavenly being. He set me back on the solid footing. He then looked at me and said two things. First, he said, "If I have you, I have Adam." In other words, "Adam will fulfill his call as long as you walk with Me. Your influence on Adam will be this significant." He then said the second thing. He said, "Many have fallen to their destruction right here." I knew he was telling me that the desire and attempt to move ahead of the timing of God would end up in devastation.

I had to wait for the "road" to be built, no matter how slow I thought the process was. I have sought to do this in the decades since. I have tried to move at the pace set by God, no matter how slow I thought it was. This is what Moses didn't do. It potentially caused a 30-year delay because of his unwise decision. His effort to do something in the flesh disrupted the timing of God.

This is one of his biggest ploys against us and God's purposes in us. Many of God's people are stuck in a place God does not intend for us to be stuck in. We must be aware of this. Otherwise, we think perhaps it wasn't God's will for us to have that which we believed we were to have. We then give up on the promises of God and try to be content where we are. We have to shake free from this and not allow it to be the normal God never intended. I always think about the people who died in that 30 extra years of captivity who didn't get to see freedom. I also think about those who were traumatized from the cruelty of bondage who might not have experienced this. So many negative things happened in the extended period of slavery that otherwise would not have occurred. This was because of an interruption of the timing of God. Somehow, the devil gained an ability to lengthen this time. Again, this is a chief endeavor of satan against the purposes of God. Nothing good comes out of the timing of God being interfered with.

Another place we see the timing of God being disrupted is in 1 Thessalonians 2:18. As spiritual and powerful as the apostle Paul was, he suffered the devil's interference with the timing of God.

Therefore we wanted to come to you—even I, Paul, time and again—but Satan hindered us.

If the devil can do this to the apostle Paul, he can do this to us. It is really easy at times to spiritualize things and just consider that it must not be what God wanted at this time. Paul didn't do this. He was honest. He said the reason they hadn't gotten to the Thessalonians was because satan interfered. The devil had successfully messed up the timing and the intent of the Lord. Sometimes the problem isn't that it's not the timing of God, it's that the devil has discovered a legal right to disrupt that timing. The result of this is hope deferred, purposes averted, and God's will frustrated.

There are some things that can give the enemy a legal right to mess with the timing of God. Let me mention just three significant ones. Unwise decisions can frustrate God's timing in matters. I have watched people make choices that were not wise, then have to live with the consequences of them. Perhaps out of their impatience, decisions were made that messed up the intentions of God. People's willful choices cause that which God desires to be lost perhaps for a long time.

Years ago, Mary and I had moved to a city to prepare for ministry. We and our first child, two months old, relocated at the word of the Lord to Tyler, Texas. This was God's chosen place for us to be made ready for what God had called us to. These were hard years. We were young and away from our families. Instead of being prepared for ministry, I was assigned to be the janitor of the church and school while holding down a full-time job. I didn't realize that God was teaching me to be a servant. All I could see was being relegated to this humbling position. My family wanted us to move back home and we were being offered ministry opportunities there, so we were considering going back.

In the midst of this, I had a dream. Understanding the dream requires that you first know we had a dog named Toby. Toby was a beautiful dog. We had brought him with us when we moved to Tyler. I let him out one morning and he never came back. I looked all over for him and could not find him. I do not know what happened to him to this very day. The fact was, his disappearance solved a problem. We were having to move from a house that had a yard for him to an apartment where he was not allowed. We did not know what we were going to do with Toby. When he disappeared, it was somewhat of a blessing in disguise. We loved him and wanted him and did everything to find him, but the problem was solved. We did move to the apartment as a young family.

It was after this that I had the dream in the midst of the struggles. In the dream, I was at my father and mother's home in the country. They had a long road that led up to their house. I was standing at the top of the road by the house and looking down the road. As I looked, I saw Toby running up the road coming toward me. This was the end of the dream. It was very short and concise, but I had a sense it meant something. I didn't know what it meant, but I knew it was important. I thought about it, pondered it, and prayed about it.

This went on for a week or so. I remember sitting at a red light, waiting to turn right to go work at the church as the janitor. As I turned, the Lord suddenly spoke clearly to me regarding the dream. With such clarity He said, "If you go back to your home, everything I delivered you from will come back to you!" Wow! Toby the dog represented what God had set me free from. He had done this when we moved to prepare for ministry. Now I was being told that if I made the decision to go back to my home, all that would come back on me. This was what Toby represented.

Needless to say, we stayed put and were equipped and prepared for the ministry we now have and have had. However, if I had made an unwise choice to leave that place, most likely my life would have taken a completely different direction. I am certain much destruction would have resulted in our life. At the very least, there would have been an interruption of the timing of God. This would have been because of an unwise decision in that moment. We must follow the leading of the Lord in our decisions. Unwise choices in these places can cause God's timing to be altered. Ephesians 5:15-17 gives us great counsel and wisdom concerning this.

> See then that you walk circumspectly, not as fools but as wise, redeeming the time, because the days are evil. Therefore do not be unwise, but understand what the will of the Lord is.

We are told to walk *circumspectly* or with exactness. In other words, we are not to divert or turn to the left or the right. We must keep our feet in the path we know has been assigned to us. We are to *redeem the time*. This literally means to *buy up the moment*. We are to invest ourselves in this time and place given to us by God. This is what the Lord was wanting me to do as the janitor of the church. I needed to invest myself in these moments of time. They were going to work in me what was needed for the decades of ministry to come. This is exactly what happened to me. If I had left this place because it was hard, I would have frustrated the timing and intent of God. It is doubtful if I would have recovered myself from those unwise decisions. If we have made unwise decisions out of fear, fleshly longing, and/or pressure and stress, we should repent. We must ask for the Lord to forgive and the devil's rights to be revoked. This can allow us to regain and recover our steps and the right paths. If we make wrong choices, God is merciful and will make a way back. We can get back into the will of God and be restored.

Another thing that can be used of the devil to disrupt the timing of God is murmuring and complaining. Our negative words empower the demonic against us. They can be used by satan to devour the purposes of God. As we saw before, 1 Corinthians 10:10 urges us not to complain and murmur.

> *Nor complain, as some of them also complained, and were destroyed by the destroyer.*

There are destructive forces released against us and our destinies when we complain. The word *complain* is the Greek word *gogguzo*. This word means "to grumble." James 5:9 tells us that something legal happens when we grumble.

> *Do not grumble against one another, brethren, lest you be condemned. Behold, the Judge is standing at the door!*

The Judge, who is God, is standing at the door. In other words, our grumbling and complaining against others can cause God to render judgments between us. It's a bad thing to grumble about a situation. It's worse to grumble and complain about a person. It can cause God to render a judgment against someone and for someone else. The word *condemned* is *katakrino*. It means "to judge against, damn, condemn." If I am speaking evil against someone else, this can cause a righteous judgment to be against me. Ezekiel 34:17-22 shows God promising to render judgments between different parts of His flock. It seems that if we are guilty of harming another part of the flock, God will come to the rescue of the injured and judge the one who has damaged.

> *And as for you, O My flock, thus says the Lord God: "Behold, I shall judge between sheep and sheep, between rams and goats. Is it too little for you to have eaten up the good pasture, that you must tread down with your feet the residue of your pasture—and to have drunk of the clear waters, that you must foul the residue with your feet? And as for My flock, they eat what you have trampled with your feet, and they drink what you have fouled with your feet." Therefore thus says the Lord God to them: "Behold, I Myself will judge between the fat and the lean sheep. Because you have pushed with side and shoulder, butted all the weak ones with your horns, and scattered them abroad, therefore I will save My flock, and they shall no longer be a prey; and I will judge between sheep and sheep."*

God promises to judge between sheep and sheep. Anyone who has been damaged and experienced ruin, God will arise to their defense. Remember, the Judge is standing at the door. I think this means not only is He hearing, but His judgment in the matter is imminent. However, if we are the ones guilty of grumbling against another, we cannot be allowed to move into the promises of God. This is what happened with the generation of the children of Israel. They were forbidden to get the inheritance intended by God. There was a loss of the initial timing of the Lord. We should repent for any place we have grumbled, complained, or held grudges against another. This can deny us that which was proposed for us. It can upset the timing of the Lord.

A third issue used to mess up the timing of God is issues in our bloodline. If there are iniquitous places in our bloodline, this can be a problem in us receiving the prophetic promises we carry. This is what happened to me. I had many prophetic promises that I personally had heard from the Lord but also had been prophesied by others as well. Yet these words were not coming to pass. Time was passing, I was getting older, and the words were not coming to fulfillment. Add to this that others who seemed inferior to me in gifting (I know this is bad to say, but I'm trying to communicate where I was) were prospering. This was all happening while I was not seeing the favor of God on my life. I was praying, seeking the Lord, seeking to live holy, and all the stuff. Yet while others who were my peers were being blessed, I was standing in a place of restraint and limits.

Before anyone corrects me, I know we are not supposed to compare ourselves with others. I'm aware of all the scriptures. Again, I'm trying to be honest about my thinking process and how I was struggling. There were prophetic words that I had carried for twenty-plus years that seemed no closer to being fulfilled than when I received them. I was definitely stuck in the old. My wife, whom I'm sure was biased, also expressed dismay at why others were being promoted ahead of me. She too wondered why I was not being favored while others were beyond me. She knew the secrets of my life. She knew the places of prayer and diligence. Yet what had been promised never came to pass.

It was at this juncture that I had one of those prophetic dreams that was to set my life on a different course. In the dream, there was a present-day judgment against me from a court because my great-great grandfather had, through negligence, injured some-body. I didn't know how or what the injury detailed. I didn't know if it was a physical injury, financial injury, or something else. I just knew he had injured someone, and because of it a court had now rendered a judgment against me. I woke up from the dream in terror. The dream was so real that as I awoke, I thought it was real in the natural. I thought I was in massive trouble because a natu-ral court had rendered a verdict against me. I remember knowing that my future was about to be massively reshaped because of this decision against me. I remember thinking that Mary and I were not going to have the future we had thought we were going to have. This judgment against me was going to change everything!

As I fully awoke, I realized it was a dream. I realized that though it wasn't real in the natural, it was real! In the spirit world and the Courts of Heaven, what my great-great grandfather had done was speaking against me. The devil was taking his negligence and using it to build a case against me. At this point, the Lord spoke to me. He said, "Your great-great grandfather, through negligence, stole the dreams of someone away. Therefore, the devil has claimed the legal right to steal your dreams away!"

This was why none of the prophetic promises were coming to pass. The devil had discovered a legal right against me to resist the purposes and prophetic promises of God in my life. For even two decades, he had successfully frustrated the timing of God. An issue in my ancestral history was being used against me to create delay and even denial. Now, however, I had the information I needed to go into the Courts of Heaven and answer this case. I immediately got out of bed and went to prayer. I began to repent for negligence in my life, my bloodline, and in particular for the negligence of my great-great grandfather. As I repented, I began to feel sorrow over what had been done to the person who had suffered because of my ancestor's negligence. I remember having a desire to bring reimbursement or recompense in some way to whoever had been hurt. Of course, I had no awareness of who that person was or who their family was. Yet my heart was to have done this if I could. I believe the desire to do that spoke before the Courts of Heaven for me. All I know is that there was an immediate shift.

Within a week, doors began to open that had never opened before. Great privileges and opportunities began to be granted. I was allowed to have new realms of influence I had never had before. This all occurred because I dealt with a bloodline issue that was creating delay and disrupting the timing of God. As we step into the Courts of Heaven by faith and operate there, the interference in the timing of God can end. We are free to move into the prophetic destiny of God. We can come out of the old and into the new!

Joel 2:25 makes a very powerful promise to us.

> *So I will restore to you the years that the swarming locust has eaten, the crawling locust, the consuming locust, and the chewing locust, My great army which I sent among you.*

God promises to reset timing for us. He promises to restore the "years" that have been lost to the disruption caused by the devil. This does not mean we get the actual years back that have already passed. Even though God can increase our days and prolong our years according to Proverbs 9:11.

> *For by me your days will be multiplied, and years of life will be added to you.*

This is wisdom speaking. Wisdom is declaring that if we walk in the wisdom of God, it can result in us seeing a multiplying of days and years being added. I take this to mean that there can be an altering of what was originally designed for us. We are told that before time began, how long we would live was preset and written in a book. Psalm 139:16 tells us this.

Your eyes saw my substance, being yet unformed. And in Your book they all were written, the days fashioned for me, when as yet there were none of them.

My days were fashioned and designed for me before I existed on earth. Things were pre-appointed for me to live out here on earth. Second Timothy 1:9 even tells me that purpose and grace were assigned to me *before time began.*

Who has saved us and called us with a holy calling, not according to our works, but according to His own purpose and grace which was given to us in Christ Jesus before time began.

My reason for existing on the earth was arranged for me before time existed. God thought me up and determined my kingdom reason and what I was to accomplish. This involved my length of life as well. However, in the scripture we saw that my days can increase and years can be added to my life if I walk in the wisdom of God! This is one of the ways years that have been eaten up can be restored to me. We should also know that if we disobey God, years previously appointed to me can be diminished. If I walk in disobedience to God's word and truth, according to Proverbs 10:27 what was originally intended for me can be lost.

The fear of the Lord prolongs days, but the years of the wicked will be shortened.

Shortened years means that what I should have gotten I did not walk in because of walking contrary to the Lord's ways. So there is an appointed length of life that is established for us. This length of life can be added to or taken from. However, when the Bible says that years shall be restored that were eaten up and consumed, it is speaking of the *productivity* of those years. God promises to give back to us the increase and production of the years that were devoured.

When Mary and I discovered the Courts of Heaven and were able to revoke the legal claims of the devil to devour, the years of loss were returned to us quickly, plus more! The stealing away of the devil through people whom we trusted unwisely was given back to us. This all occurred because there was a resetting of time and a recovery of all that was lost! We came out of the years of the old and into the new that God had arranged for us. The devil's right to afflict us and destroy our future was annulled. The result has been blessings and increase on every side. We are living out one of my most favorite scriptures found in Ecclesiastes 5:20.

For he will not dwell unduly on the days of his life, because God keeps him busy with the joy of his heart.

We are not worried about our present days or the ones to come. God is keeping us busy with the joy of our heart. We are loving life and seeing good days. We have stepped out of the old places of life and pain. We have stepped into the new places of joy and expectation of good. You can too. The Courts of Heaven will move you from old to new and into the goodness of the Lord!

Thank You, Lord, for the privilege of accessing Your Courts.
As I stand before You as the righteousness of God in Christ
Jesus, I ask that any disruption of timing in my life will

be recovered. *May every loss and every frustration created by this be restored. Thank You that You have promised a restoring of at least the productivity of years. I receive this in Jesus' Name. May it be recorded that I repent of unwise decisions, of grumbling against others, and of bloodline issues before You. May Your blood of sprinkling now speak for me. Let every legal claim of the devil to interrupt Your timing now be revoked. Bring me out of the old I have been held in and into the new ordained by You for me. May Your passions for me be fulfilled in Jesus' Name, amen.*

CHAPTER 6

The Essential of Faith

As I mentioned in a previous chapter, there are those who are critics of the Courts of Heaven teaching. One of their criticisms is that I am guilty of Gnosticism. Gnosticism comes from the Greek word *gnosis.* This is the word for *knowledge.* The critics claim I teach that you need to have special knowledge to operate in the Courts of Heaven. Nothing can be further from the truth! As I have stated before, if everyone can't operate in the Courts of Heaven, then no one should or can!

The Court of Heaven is a spiritual dimension that we enter through the blood of the Lamb. Jesus gave us access into these spiritual dimensions by His offering on the cross and the empowerment of the Holy Spirit. We have been granted access into these unseen places that affect and control the seen dimensions. With this said, you do not need special knowledge to function in these places. You simply need to operate in faith.

When I first encountered the Courts of Heaven, I was led to believe you needed a *seer or high-level prophetic person* to help you navigate these realms. I didn't know any better, so I thought this to be true. Quite honestly, some of these seers could get really strange and weird. I had a problem theologically with what some of them were *seeing*. Yet because of my initial encounter in these realms, I thought this was necessary. Let me also say that I had *help* from some seers who were quite beneficial. I am not condemning this gifting at all. I just have a problem with those who create theology from what they see and not from what the Bible says. For instance, I had one person tell me a certain spiritual dimension was not connected to the Courts of Heaven. This was based on what a seer in his life had told him they had seen in the spiritual realm. I then took the word of God and showed him that this realm was in fact a part of the Courts of Heaven. He then had a problem. Was he going to believe what the seer said or what the word of God said? The truth is, this is happening in the church quite a bit. This is why God has ordained apostles to establish doctrine and not prophets. Acts 2:42 lets us know that the church walked in the *apostles' doctrine.* This is because apostles create doctrine from the word of God, not from some spiritual experience they are having.

And they continued steadfastly in the apostles' doctrine and fellowship, in the breaking of bread, and in prayers.

With this said, what is seen and prophetically understood can be of great value in confirming the word of God. For instance, I was teaching in Germany and my translator was a seer. I did not know this. As I taught, I wondered if I should teach on how to bring offerings to the altar of the Lord. This is a function of a house of prayer. We see this in Isaiah 56:7.

> *Even them I will bring to My holy mountain, and make*
> *them joyful in My house of prayer. Their burnt offerings*
> *and their sacrifices will be accepted on My altar; for My*
> *house shall be called a house of prayer for all nations.*

We are to mix our prayers as a house with our offerings upon the Lord's altar. I honestly decided they were not ready to process this portion of the Courts of Heaven. As we finished up the session, the translator looked at me during the break and said to me, "What are the fiery stones?" I knew what she was asking because of Ezekiel 28:14.

> *You were the anointed cherub who covers; I established you;*
> *you were on the holy mountain of God; you walked back*
> *and forth in the midst of fiery stones.*

I said to her, "Why are you asking?"

She said, "Because we are standing on them." She said, "I'm seeing them as you're teaching."

I thought, *This is amazing!* I had not mentioned this realm at all in my teaching. She had never heard of it, yet she was seeing it. She had no idea of what I was debating in my mind. I didn't have any awareness that she was a seer. I thought she was simply a translator hired to help me communicate the teaching on the Courts of Heaven. Yet here she was, a clearly reliable seer, seeing into the unseen world. She was seeing the altar of the Lord where our offerings were to be brought as a House of Prayer. We did teach on this realm and saw great breakthroughs come. I wouldn't have even gone that direction without this seer letting me know *where* we were in the spirit world.

I appreciate real seers and prophetic people and their abilities that can help influence and even direct. However, this does not replace simple faith in the word of God. I am not a seer on that level. I do see some. However, my prophetic abilities are more as a feeler and a hearer than as a seer. I have learned to use these prophetic skills in the Courts of Heaven to get breakthrough. However, the biggest thing I do is move in faith in the Courts of Heaven. This means I take the word of God and simply believe it and step into it. Without seeing angels or other heavenly dimensions, I get massive breakthrough. I do this by simply believing what the word of God teaches and moving in agreement with it. This is faith.

You don't have to be weird or strange to operate in the Courts of Heaven. In fact, the more you do it, the more natural it becomes. So what are some principles to moving by faith in the Courts of Heaven? First of all, we should believe this realm exists. We do this because of its revelation in Daniel 7:9-10. This judicial system is revealed and seen there by Daniel the prophet. I don't have to *see it* to know it exists. Daniel saw it.

> *I watched till thrones were put in place, and the Ancient of Days was seated; His garment was white as snow, and the hair of His head was like pure wool. His throne was a fiery flame, its wheels a burning fire; a fiery stream issued and came forth from before Him. A thousand thousands ministered to Him; ten thousand times ten thousand stood before Him. The court was seated, and the books were opened.*

My faith has its roots in what is recorded in the word of God through a prophet of the Lord. This is what we are told we are to do. Second Peter 1:20-21 establishes the authority of scriptures given prophetically.

Knowing this first, that no prophecy of Scripture is of any private interpretation, for prophecy never came by the will of man, but holy men of God spoke as they were moved by the Holy Spirit.

All the New Testament scriptures' foundation is the Old Testament scriptures. In other words, Peter is letting us know we can place confidence and faith in what the Old Testament prophets saw and revealed. When I enter the Courts of Heaven by faith, it is based on what the written word of God has revealed.

A second principle to operating in faith in the Courts of Heaven is confidence in Jesus' blood to grant me access. Hebrews 12:24 lets me know that Jesus' blood is presently speaking for me. This blood grants me access into the Courts.

To Jesus the Mediator of the new covenant, and to the blood of sprinkling that speaks better things than that of Abel.

Abel's blood cried for vengeance and punishment of Cain who had killed him. However, Jesus' blood cries for mercy, forgiveness, redemption, and reconciliation. Jesus' blood, which has been sprinkled on the mercy seat in Heaven, is speaking and testifying for us. The testimony of Jesus' sprinkled blood gives God the legal right to forgive and redeem! I am worthy to step into the holiest of places in the spirit because of what Jesus' blood is presently saying about me.

A third means of moving in faith is to pay attention to what you are sensing. Hebrews 11:1 tells us that faith is believing what you sense more than what you see.

Now faith is the substance of things hoped for, the evidence of things not seen.

When I say "see" here, I am speaking of the natural world. As we step into the Courts of Heaven, we should be aware of movement in the unseen realm. Therefore, I am sensing and moving in agreement with those realities. Quite honestly, I never cease to be amazed at what happens when I operate this way. For instance, as I move in agreement with what I sense, I'm quite often shocked by things that transpire. My operating in concert with what I initially feel, sense, hear, and even see seems to unlock other realms. It's much like Moses at the burning bush in Exodus 3:2-5. The moment Moses moved toward what he was seeing, God spoke to him.

> *And the Angel of the Lord appeared to him in a flame of fire from the midst of a bush. So he looked, and behold, the bush was burning with fire, but the bush was not consumed. Then Moses said, "I will now turn aside and see this great sight, why the bush does not burn."*
>
> *So when the Lord saw that he turned aside to look, God called to him from the midst of the bush and said, "Moses, Moses!"*
>
> *And he said, "Here I am."*
>
> *Then He said, "Do not draw near this place. Take your sandals off your feet, for the place where you stand is holy ground."*

Moses' movement in faith unlocked a whole realm and encounter with God. My advice is just move! This can lead you into great places of breakthrough that are unimaginable. Take a step of faith and begin to encounter and function in the Courts of Heaven.

Lord, I come to Your Courts. Thank You for any and all gifting You have granted me prophetically. I will use them and be faithful to steward them. However, I will move in simple faith in Your Courts, taking You at Your word. I will believe in all that Your blood has done for me and the access it grants me in Your Courts. I come to function in this realm as Your servant and the righteousness of God in Christ Jesus. Help me, I pray, in my weakness to navigate fully in this realm of the Spirit by faith. In Jesus' Name, amen.

CHAPTER 7

Prophetically Inspired

We all have prophetic abilities—especially if you are filled/ baptized in the Holy Spirit. These prophetic abilities can be of great help and benefit when operating in the Courts of Heaven. John 16:13 gives us insight into the Holy Spirit and His nature.

However, when He, the Spirit of truth, has come, He will guide you into all truth; for He will not speak on His own authority, but whatever He hears He will speak; and He will tell you things to come.

Notice that when He speaks, He speaks what another says and He tells us about things to come. This means the very nature of the Spirit of God is prophetic. If the Holy Spirit lives in us, then the prophetic nature of God is in us as well. I want to encourage you to stop saying you are not prophetic or don't have prophetic abilities. Your voice and words work against you.

I remember being in another nation and praying with a group that was in great distress. Before we began to pray, I told them, "I do not see." What I meant by this was I'm not a seer; therefore, don't expect that of me. As I later considered what motivated me to say this, I saw that it was born of insecurities and uncertainties of who I was. Then after we had prayer and I had received some very significant revelation concerning their situation, they were commenting on how it helped them. I then began to make light of my abilities because I felt uncomfortable with the affirmation they were giving. At that moment, the Lord said to me, "Stop saying that!" I knew the Lord was correcting me. He began to convict and chasten me with my treatment of what was coming from Him. He showed me that I was devaluing His gifting in my life. He showed me that if this gifting was to grow, I needed to treat it as holy. My not treasuring what was from Him was an actual offense to Him. This is one of the ways we *grieve* the Holy Spirit. Ephesians 4:30 exhorts us to be careful to not hurt and offend the Spirit of God.

And do not grieve the Holy Spirit of God, by whom you were sealed for the day of redemption.

The word *grieve* in the Greek is *lupeo*. It means "to be in distress, heaviness, to make sorrowful." This is what I was doing by diminishing the gifting of the Lord in me. Out of my insecurity and sense of inferiority, I was offending the Spirit of the Lord. I remember excusing myself and walking to another part of the room. I began to repent for my serious error. I promised the Lord I would not do this again. I would instead value and regard the giftings of God and seek to develop them. The result has been that I have increased in my prophetic abilities. It has greatly helped me in my function in the Courts of Heaven. It has allowed me to step out of the old and into the new.

For instance, delay has always been something that has sought to attach itself to me. I successfully dealt with it on a certain level, but it tried to reattach to me later on. There were a couple of opportunities that had been promised to me. However, actual occurrence had not happened. The history of delay in my life made me worry that they would not happen. I was in a hotel room and simply said to the Lord, "Is there something yet resisting me in the spirit world?"

Without hesitation, the Lord seemed to say, "Yes, there is." The truth is that I could have dismissed this as my imagination and questioned whether it was really the Lord. However, I treated it instantly like it was. The result was the Lord started speaking to me. Just like we shared in the last chapter about Moses, my movement unlocked an encounter with God that brought tremendous breakthrough. As a result of my faith to embrace this whisper of the Lord, I then felt I heard the Lord say, "I need for you to say before Me what Moses said when Korah accused him." As the Lord said this, I remembered that Moses in Numbers 16:15 renounced the idea that he had taken something from someone.

> *Then Moses was very angry, and said to the Lord, "Do not respect their offering. I have not taken one donkey from them, nor have I hurt one of them."*

I realized that there was an accusation in the Courts of Heaven against me that I had stolen something that belonged to someone else. I knew that I wasn't guilty of this, yet somebody in the natural was speaking these things about me. The devil was taking their words of accusation and using it against me in the Courts of Heaven. These words were causing delay to occur in my life. I understood this from a prophetic standpoint. I then *knew* intuitively that if I said what the Lord told me to say, it would give God the legal right to *look* into the books of Heaven to verify what I was saying. There are all sorts of books in Heaven. This is why Daniel 7:10 tells us the Court is seated and the books, plural, are opened.

A fiery stream issued And came forth from before Him. A thousand thousands ministered to Him; ten thousand times ten thousand stood before Him. The court was seated, and the books were opened.

Everything is written down and recorded in the books of Heaven. The Jewish people believe that even our thoughts are written down. We know that our words are recorded. This is because according to Matthew 12:36-37 we will give an account for every idle word we have spoken.

But I say to you that for every idle word men may speak, they will give account of it in the day of judgment. For by your words you will be justified, and by your words you will be condemned.

If we are to give an account in the day of judgment, then these words must be recorded somewhere! They are written in the books of Heaven. If words are recorded, then there must be books in Heaven that are recording everything concerning us and our activities.

I was aware that as I said what the Lord told me to say, it was granting God the right to investigate these books. The books revealed that I was not guilty of what was being said about me. This allowed the Lord to render a decision on my behalf. The words being spoken against me, accusing me of taking something that wasn't mine, were now annulled. I felt a tremendous release as I prophetically walked through this process. I thought that maybe I had dealt with that which was causing a delay. I didn't know that the prophetic process still had a necessary piece to be accomplished.

As I returned home the next day or so, I had a dream on that night. In my dream, Mary and I were standing before this very well-known minister. In the natural, I have no connection to this ministry. I've never supported them. I've never attended a meeting. I've only seen him on television a handful of times. In fact, I don't even really enjoy his ministry. In the dream, however, as we were standing before his ministry, and we were deciding how much money we were going to give to his ministry. Mary said, "Let's give $100." I said in response, "No, let's give $1,000." This was the end of the dream. When I woke up, I knew immediately what I was supposed to be doing. I was supposed to give this ministry $1,000 so that the money would *speak* for me in the Courts. I had this *knowing* that the activity in the hotel room had silenced the voice against me in the Courts, but I needed something speaking for me also. This comes from my knowledge that money has a voice in the Courts of Heaven. Hebrews 7:8 is clear that our tithe speaks for us in the heavenly realm.

Here mortal men receive tithes, but there he receives them, of whom it is witnessed that he lives.

The writer of Hebrews is making a distinction concerning bringing tithes to the Levitical priesthood and the Melchizedek order. Jesus is our High Priest after the order of Melchizedek. Therefore, we honor His priesthood with our tithe. Notice that when we do this, there is a *witness released on our behalf.* The word *witness* is the Greek word *matureo.* This word means "to give testimony, to be a witness judicially." Therefore, when we give our tithes, Jesus receives them as our High Priest. This tithe is releasing testimony that we believe He lives. This testimony connects us to His present-day life and activity on our behalf. We are told that Jesus is alive and interceding for us. When we bring our tithe, the witness on our behalf joins us to His present-day ministry for us. This is because your money has a voice/testimony in the Courts of Heaven. We also know this is true because of Matthew 5:23-26.

> *Therefore if you bring your gift to the altar, and there remember that your brother has something against you, leave your gift there before the altar, and go your way. First be reconciled to your brother, and then come and offer your gift. Agree with your adversary quickly, while you are on the way with him, lest your adversary deliver you to the judge, the judge hand you over to the officer, and you be thrown into prison. Assuredly, I say to you, you will by no means get out of there till you have paid the last penny.*

Jesus is clear that we are not to bring our offering if there are problems in our heart. This is because the wrong testimony coming from our offerings will result in judgments against us from the Courts of Heaven. The devil will take advantage of the words against us from our offering and build a case that is adverse to us. The result will be a decision against us that can result in us being thrown into prison. This is why we are told that we should make sure things are reconciled before bringing an offering. Otherwise, our offering will be tainted with a wrong witness. It will be speaking against us in the Courts of Heaven rather than for us.

Notice that we are then judged and end up in prison. This is all based on the testimony of our gift. The other scripture that is so powerful is Malachi 3:3-5. This scripture unveils the power of a right offering speaking for us and even the culture we are a part of.

> *He will sit as a refiner and a purifier of silver; He will purify the sons of Levi, and purge them as gold and silver, That they may offer to the Lord An offering in righteousness.*
> *"Then the offering of Judah and Jerusalem will be pleasant to the Lord, As in the days of old, As in former years. And I will come near you for judgment; I will be a swift witness against sorcerers, against adulterers, against perjurers, against those who exploit wage earners and widows and orphans, and against those who turn away an alien— Because they do not fear Me," says the Lord of hosts.*

This portion of scripture is declaring the power of our offerings to bring testimony before the Lord. This testimony will cause God to judge that which is afflicting society. Our offerings are mighty witnesses in the Courts of Heaven. They not only speak on behalf of us but also on behalf of the culture we represent before the Lord. When this occurs, the testimony God needs to render righteous judgments is provided. When I bring my offering as a part of the House of Prayer, these offerings speak for our culture as well as for us as individuals. This is why God can render judgments against what is afflicting society based on the witness of our offerings before Him.

This is what I knew concerning the dream I had about bringing an offering to this high-profile ministry. I considered and thought about this dream all day after I had it. That night, Mary went to bed and I was still up. I started flipping through the television channels. As I turned the channels, I came upon this ministry that I had dreamed about. Only because of the dream did I turn to this channel. As I did, the main man and another guy were speaking. They were raising money. They were saying, "We are asking you to give $1,000. However, if you can't do this, then give a tithe of that and give $100." As I heard this, I thought, *That's my dream.* That was all I needed. Any reluctance to sow $1,000 into this ministry was gone. I went to my computer, found this ministry, and sent the $1,000 to them immediately. It was 11 p.m. when I sent the money. I had fulfilled what I had been prophetically told to do.

The next morning at 10 p.m., my phone rang. It was the people I had been waiting on to get back with me. The end result was that things were arranged and I was given a worldwide influence that still exists to this day. As a result of listening and moving prophetically, I had operated in the Courts of Heaven. I had silenced the voices against me and released voices to speak for me. The result has been a wide open door to a great effect in the nations of the earth. God is faithful and true to His word. He will allow us to move with Him when we operate in the prophetic realms. It is not beyond us. We all have these abilities and giftings on some level. Start using them today.

Lord, I come before You as the Judge of all the earth. I thank You for the prophetic abilities You have granted me as a Spirit-filled believer. I receive the prophetic nature of the Holy Spirit who lives in me. I repent for any devaluing of the prophetic gifting in me, because it doesn't "look" like that in someone else. I honor Your gifting in me. I treasure that which You have trusted me with. I purposely stir up these giftings. I ask that I might use these to function in the Courts of Heaven on a higher level. May this function move me from the old and into the new. I pay attention to the revelation You bring to me from these prophetic places. In Jesus' Name, amen.

CHAPTER 8

Discerning What Is in the Books

Unlocking the new that God has for us requires us discerning what is in the books of Heaven. As we have said, there are many books in Heaven. There are many different kinds of books in Heaven. However, one of the main books is the book of destiny. We have already looked at Psalm 139:16 earlier. This is a critical scripture to understanding books and what is in them.

> *Your eyes saw my substance, being yet unformed. And in Your book they all were written, the days fashioned for me, when as yet there were none of them.*

David the psalmist gives insight into how our kingdom purpose was established. There are several things about this scripture that we should look into. Through prophetic revelation, we can discern what is contained in the book that has our God-ordained destiny and future in it. This is critical to getting out of the old and into the new. Whatever *new* God has for you is written in the book about you. I remember several years ago being in the meeting of a prophet. As the meeting was progressing and worship was happening, this prophet walked over to me. He said he was seeing my book that was opened. He said the pages were turning very fast. He understood that the delay in my life was being overcome. He further declared that God was catching me up in my destiny and purpose. This was why the pages of the book were rapidly being turned forward. Every resistance was removed. I had been freed to come out of the old I was stuck in and into the new! This has in fact happened.

If we are to discern what is written in the books about us, we should understand some significant things. Let's look at truths and facts about these books of destiny. First of all, the Bible called this book "Yours." This is referring to God. David said what was written in the book was about God's agenda and purpose. This is God's book. So often we major on our desire, purpose, and destiny. The truth is, it's about Him. According to Romans 11:36, everything is about Him and for Him.

For of Him and through Him and to Him are all things, to whom be glory forever. Amen.

This is essential to being the most effective in the Courts of Heaven. What we are doing foremost in the Courts is contending for His will to be done. This is what the devil ultimately is resisting. Our commission as His people on earth is to fight for God's will to be done on earth, even as it is in heaven. Of course, this is what Jesus taught us to pray in Matthew 6:10.

Your kingdom come. Your will be done on earth as it is in heaven.

Anything and everything resisting the will of God on earth, we are to remove and revoke its rights. It is our job to see what it written in the books fleshed out on earth. The book is the Lord's and contains His passion and desire on earth. Another thing about the book is it is what God *saw. God saw my substance yet unformed.* Clearly this is what is written in the book of Heaven about me. The Lord looked down through the ages and *saw* that which concerned me. The Lord methodically has pieced together His design and plan for the ages. He has purposed that it will require generations to fulfill His redemptive plan on earth. This means that different people will have different assignments in each generation. This will allow the redemptive purposes of God to be fulfilled on earth. Revelation 10:7 proclaims the mystery of God finished. This is the redemptive plan of God that will be fully accomplished.

But in the days of the sounding of the seventh angel, when he is about to sound, the mystery of God would be finished, as He declared to His servants the prophets.

Everything that God has purposed and planned will be fully unveiled and completed. Each one of us has a part to play in this plan. This is what is written in His book. God looked down through the ages and saw a hole or lack in His plan. You were thought up as one who would fill that hole and provide for the lack. You are the answer—a piece necessary to God's plan. God saw a need and purposed to meet it through creating you. He saw you and everything you would need to be. He then wrote this down in the book.

Another thing we should know about the books of destiny is your substance was written in this book. This is a reference to your DNA. This is what makes you good at certain things and not good at others. This is what makes you gravitate toward certain things while you are repelled from others. This is even what makes you like and join yourself to certain people while you may not be drawn to others. Biblically speaking, this is determined by a grace you were given before time began. We've looked at it earlier, but 2 Timothy 1:9 gives us insight into this.

> *Who has saved us and called us with a holy calling, not according to our works, but according to His own purpose and grace which was given to us in Christ Jesus before time began.*

Notice that purpose and grace was given to us before time began. This means that we were born with certain propensities, inclinations, and even giftings. These are clues to the destiny in the purposes of God we were created for. Whatever our destinies are, connected to the purpose of God, we were made with giftings and inclinations in that area. We should pay attention to these. They are signs to our ultimate purpose and intent.

The other thing we should realize about our books is the days have been fashioned beforehand. This means at least a couple of things. One is it implies our lifespan and length of days is already determined. As we said before, this seems to be somewhat able to be altered. It can be diminished or increased. However, it would appear that from before time we were appointed a certain number of days. Our days being fashioned can also mean that there is an appointed time in our lifespan when certain significant things happen. In other words, there are times when strategic things occur as we step into new seasons of our destiny arranged by God. These are *kairos* moments of time. *Kairos* is a Greek word for time. It means a moment in time when opportunities are granted to enter divine purposes. These times should not be missed or refused. These are times when it is the season God has planned and prepared you for. This is when things accelerate into the next place that God has predetermined. These days have already been fashioned for you.

With all this said, we must prophetically sense what is written in our book. This means out of our walk with God, we are able to discern what we were made for. The more intimately we walk with the Lord, the more He is able to unveil for us what we are ultimately here for. I remember years ago, as I was praying, I heard the Lord say, "You will disciple nations." This was when I was in a great time of distress. People were against me and things looked very bleak. I also heard the Lord in this time say, "They do not determine your future, I do." These were significant words. I now know those words came out of my book that is in Heaven. I was prophetically hearing what was connected to my book. These words have come to pass and still continue to come to pass. These were not things I chose for myself, but what God wrote in my book before time began. He gave me giftings, inclinations, propensities, and desires consistent with what is in my book. These have helped me discern what I am called to. As I have contended in the Courts of Heaven, I have seen every delay revoked. I have been able to recover myself and see the purposes of God written in my book be fulfilled. You can too.

Lord, I know that Your purpose is connected to my destiny
You wrote in Your book about me. I declare before You that
I desire this destiny that Your purpose might be done. I ask
that I might have all that is written in Your book about

me. I ask that every delay would be revoked and removed. Any legal thing that the enemy might be using against me, I ask that it be annulled. I want the fullness of all that You wrote about me to become mine. Let Your purposes be fulfilled on earth. Let satan's agenda be undone and Your will be accomplished, in Jesus' Name, amen.

CHAPTER 9

Necessary Grace

As we saw in the last chapter, grace is absolutely necessary to moving from the old and into the new. In fact, the receiving of new dimensions of grace will propel us from the old places and into the new ones planned for us. I've noticed through the years that grace moves us from one level of living into another.

For instance, our move to Colorado Springs, Colorado, from Waco, Texas, involved a new level of grace being imparted. We had lived in Colorado Springs from 2007 until 2013. We then moved back to Texas so I could be an adjunct professor at Christ For the Nations Institute. I thought that our time in Colorado was finished. I had loved living there, but simply thought that was a season that was over. Then, while living in Waco and finishing the assignment there, I had a dream. In the dream I was in Colorado Springs, Colorado. I had invited my friend Dutch Sheets to come to this location to consult with me on a book I was going to write. As the consultation on the book ended, in the dream Dutch looked at me and said, "Are you going to move back here?"

I responded, "I don't know, Dutch."

He then looked at me and began to prophesy to me. He said, "This time, by the grace of God, you will live at a higher level."

The first time we lived in Colorado Springs, we were under great demonic assault. There were unfounded and unwarranted attacks against my character. Our adult children were making bad and wrong choices. Our finances were under assault. Pretty much anything and everything you can imagine was going wrong. I had been told before I moved there that anyone apostolic and/or prophetic would encounter this. The hierarchy of demonic rule in that city would come after anyone who had this apostolic/prophetic call on their life. I was told that I would need to get this thing under authority, or it would harass me and my family's life.

I found this to be true. We were under constant barrage for several years during our time there. We then moved back to Texas in the scenario I have described. Now, it seemed I was being told as I was to move back to Colorado Springs. However, this time I would, by the *grace of God,* live at a higher level.

We did make this transition. The Lord went ahead of us and we ended up moving back to Colorado Springs. A house was secured that was what we would desire. There is definitely a grace on Mary and me both that was not there before. We are *living at a higher level.* This seems to mean that what touched us before is not able to touch us now. We have been positioned in the spirit realm at a place that the devil cannot touch us, whereas before he had access to us.

Now, he cannot touch us because the grace of God has positioned us to live at another place in the spirit.

Of course, Colorado Springs is positioned right next to Pike's Peak. This is a looming peak that the city sits under the shadow of. When you look at this mountain, you can see the tree line. In other words, there is a visible place where trees stop growing as you ascend the mountain. It is known that above this line there are no snakes. They are unable to survive at that altitude. In the spirit realm, we are to live above the snake line. This is what it seems God was saying to me. I would, by the grace of God, be able to live above where the snakes are! I have been positioned above that place.

This is not a place we can attain on our own. At least it's not a place I had been able to arrive at. However, as I agreed and came into alignment with God's will about living in Colorado Springs, there was a grace awaiting me that I could step into. This grace propelled me into a new level of function and living in which the demon powers cannot attack me. Living at a higher level speaks of another realm of authority that powers of darkness must acknowledge and regard. This clearly has been given to me because of the grace of God imparted to my life.

The apostle Paul declared in 1 Corinthians 15:10 that what he was, he became by the grace of God.

> *But by the grace of God I am what I am, and His grace toward me was not in vain; but I labored more abundantly than they all, yet not I, but the grace of God which was with me.*

It is the grace of God that makes us and transforms us into what God needs us to be. Remember that there are different versions of grace according to 1 Peter 4:10. The grace of God is a varied thing that produces different effects in different people's lives. Based on the kind of grace we have received, we can and will function differently than others.

As each one has received a gift, minister it to one another, as good stewards of the manifold grace of God.

The kind of grace you have received determines the kind of gift you carry. The word *manifold* is the Greek word *poikilos*. It means "motley, various in character." In other words, the grace of God has varying demonstrations attached to it. Our calling in God determines the kind of grace we receive. As a result of my calling to Colorado Springs, the grace of God allows me to live at a high level in the spirit realm of the city. This gives me an authority over the powers of darkness so that they cannot touch me or my family. It also grants me an authority from which to function in the spirit world. I am able to fulfill the assignments of God because of the grace of God that is on my life.

The thing that allowed this grace to come on me was my obedience to the Lord's word. Only by moving to Colorado Springs was I able to step into this grace. If I had not moved to that place, I wouldn't have received that grace. My obedience to the will of God allowed me a place in the grace of God. This is what James 4:6-7 reveals to us. As we humble ourselves in obedience, grace comes that causes us to overcome the devil.

But He gives more grace. Therefore He says: "God resists the proud, But gives grace to the humble." Therefore submit to God. Resist the devil and he will flee from you.

When we submit ourselves to the will of God, more grace comes on our lives. The result is an authority to resist the devil and see him flee. It is the grace of God on our life that gives us this new place of authority and power. We are able to live at a higher level.

In actuality, it is activity in the Courts of Heaven that grants us these new dimensions of grace. I believe that when I chose to obey God's word, it allowed God from His Courts to legally deposit into my life new realms of grace. This causes me to function at a higher level in Colorado Springs.

Colorado Springs has always had a spiritual governmental call on it. What I mean by this is there is a place in the spirit that God intends for it to occupy. There are certain places and cities where this is true. Jerusalem is a city that was ordained by God to be a source of His authority into the earth. As a result of this *call,* there has always been great warfare over and for this city. There has been a contention concerning who will possess and control this city. Even when all the land of Canaan was taken by Joshua, the city of Jerusalem was never permanently taken. In the days of David, the city was still possessed and controlled by the Jebusites. However, David and his mighty men were able to take this seemingly unconquerable city. Second Samuel 5:5-10 shows David and his mighty men defeating the Jebusites and possessing the city of Jerusalem.

> *In Hebron he reigned over Judah seven years and six months, and in Jerusalem he reigned thirty-three years over all Israel and Judah.*
>
> *And the king and his men went to Jerusalem against the Jebusites, the inhabitants of the land, who spoke to David, saying, "You shall not come in here; but the blind and the lame will repel you," thinking, "David cannot come in here."*

Nevertheless David took the stronghold of Zion (that is, the City of David).

Now David said on that day, "Whoever climbs up by way of the water shaft and defeats the Jebusites (the lame and the blind, who are hated by David's soul), he shall be chief and captain." Therefore they say, "The blind and the lame shall not come into the house."

Then David dwelt in the stronghold, and called it the City of David. And David built all around from the Millo and inward. So David went on and became great, and the Lord God of hosts was with him.

The Jebusites considered their position in this city to be impenetrable. Therefore, they made the boast that even lame and blind people could keep David and his men out. However, David and his men took this city. Notice that after David took the city of Jerusalem, he built it and became great. In other words, the taking of the city for the kingdom purposes of God was a key to the future God had for David. I believe there are yet cities that God wants *taken* for His purposes. However, God needs men and women after His own heart whom he can trust and use for these purposes. Remember, this was the nature and character of David. Acts 13:22 declares that David had a heart after the Lord. God could trust him.

And when He had removed him, He raised up for them David as king, to whom also He gave testimony and said, "I have found David the son of Jesse, a man after My own heart, who will do all My will."

God removed Saul and replaced him with David. He did this because David's heart was after the Lord. When God finds one whose heart is after the Lord, He will trust him with much. David and his mighty men subdued Jerusalem. They set up an expression of the kingdom of God through this city. God is still looking for this today.

Where are the men and women of God whom God can empower for such things? May they be found so that cities might become expressions of His kingdom rule on earth. I believe there are cities that God wants to grace people to impact. This will allow them to step out of the old and into the new. It will be the grace of God that empowers them to move into these new places arranged by God for them. These new deposits of His grace into His people will result in new levels of function and life.

As I stand before Your Courts, Lord, I ask for new levels of grace that will transition me from the old to the new. Thank You that Your grace empowers me to move forward. It will cause me to be unstuck and propel me into the next places that You have for me. I receive more grace for this transition into my life. I also ask for transformation of whatever sphere You have called me to. May that which I have authority over become an expression of the kingdom of God—even the city You have placed me in. I want to fulfill my kingdom assignment as a result of Your grace placed on my life. In Jesus' Name, amen.

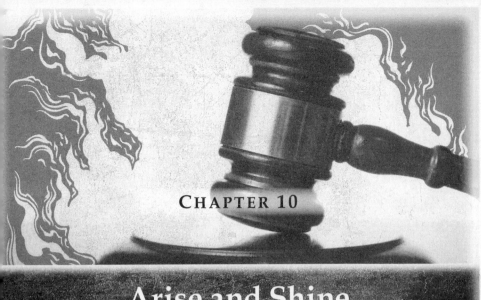

CHAPTER 10

Arise and Shine

Sometimes, our feeling of being stuck is not because things haven't been arranged in the spirit world. Sometimes, it is because we have not moved in faith to step into what has already been set into place. Isaiah 60:1 tells us that we must arise into the glory that has already been released.

> *Arise, shine; for your light has come! And the glory of the Lord is risen upon you.*

This prophetic declaration is telling us that something of the favor of God has *already come*. We are told that the glory of the Lord has *already risen* on us. The reason we are not experiencing what this implies is because we have not chosen to *arise and shine!*

Sometimes we have to act like we have it before we might think we do. As we do, we discover we have been unstuck. This can be because our operation in the Courts of Heaven has in fact accomplished much. I remember years ago, when I planted the church in Waco, we had grown to around 150 but were stuck there for several years. For these years, we had been praying daily for breakthrough, increase, and harvest. However, we were at the same place. I was speaking to a group one afternoon. As I stood before these people, I suddenly heard the Lord say, "If you will sow, I will give you a harvest."

At that moment, I realized we had done all the work that was necessary in the spirit world for a harvest. However, we had not functionally and practically sown seed to reach people for Jesus. We were in our facility, having good services, prayers, and worship, but there was no practical effort to reach the lost. God was saying to me that the work was done in the spirit world, and had probably been done for a long time. It was now time to sow. We then chose to *arise and shine*. The result of all our praying, when mixed with sowing, brought a harvest. We very quickly went from the 150 in attendance to over 600. This happened because the work had been done in the spirit world but had to have the natural aspect of sowing added to it.

We must believe that things have shifted in the unseen realm and are ready for us to succeed. When we believe our light has come and the glory has risen on us, we will step into that place and get unstuck! I want to encourage you that if you have done the work, believe and arise and shine. You will see all that God promised you start to unfold. This will occur because you have been effective in the Courts of Heaven and your day has come!

I come before Your Courts, Lord, and I ask that I would have the wisdom to arise and shine. Thank You that what You have promised me is now ready to manifest. The work is done in the Courts in the spirit world. I now by faith move into all that has been assured me. Thank You for Your faithfulness. May I see the fullness of that which has been promised as I stand before You in these days. In Jesus' Name, amen.

About Robert Henderson

Robert Henderson is a global apostolic leader who operates in revelation and impartation. His teaching empowers the body of Christ to see the hidden truths of scripture clearly and apply them for breakthrough results. Driven by a mandate to disciple nations through writing and speaking, Robert travels extensively around the globe, teaching on the apostolic, the Kingdom of God, the "Seven Mountains," and most notably, the Courts of Heaven. He has been married to Mary for 40 years. They have six children and five grandchildren. Together they are enjoying life in beautiful Colorado Springs, Colorado.

From

Robert Henderson

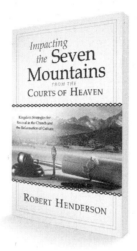

Robert Henderson started to explore the question, "what would the seven mountains of culture look like in a reformed state?" There is much talk in the apostolic and prophetic community about reformation and transformation, but sometimes, we don't have a clear vision of what it would actually look like for these spheres of influence to be modeled, shaped, and impacted by believers who carry the Kingdom of God into their everyday places of assignment.

As the bestselling teacher and leading authority on the *Courts of Heaven*, Robert Henderson explores each of the seven mountains of influence—religion, arts and entertainment, media, business, government, family, and education—and gives a powerful vision of what each one *could* look like if it were transformed and served by the Kingdom of God.

However, in order to see principalities broken and ruling spiritual forces dismantled, we must do more than pray standard warfare prayers; we must enter the Courts of Heaven to contend for Kingdom influence and impact!

Purchase your copy wherever books are sold

From

Robert Henderson

Begin Your Supernatural Journey into the Courts of Heaven

What does it mean to make your case in the Courts of Heaven? In recent years, God has raised up Robert Henderson as a prophetic voice, calling Christians to pursue breakthrough by using the Courts of Heaven prayer blueprint.

In this all-new message, Henderson gives you practical keys that will enable you to boldly access the Courts of Heaven and state your prayer cases with confidence.

You will:

- Understand the three dimensions of prayer.
- Discover the 3 keys to unlocking your breakthrough in the Courts of Heaven.
- Learn the 6 prophetic declarations that Jesus' blood makes on your behalf.
- Cancel the devil's accusations by releasing the supernatural power of your testimony.

Learn how to access the Courts of Heaven, make your case, and watch as prayers are answered, miracles are released, and long-awaited break-throughs come to fruition!

Purchase your copy wherever books are sold

From
Robert Henderson

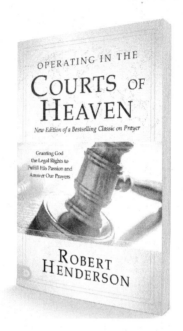

Present Your Case Before the Courts of Heaven...
and Receive Breakthrough!

Operating in the Courts of Heaven has become an international bestseller that has supernaturally transformed lives all over the world. It's not another prayer strategy; it's a blueprint for engaging a spiritual dimension called the Courts of Heaven. Robert Henderson biblically teaches believers how to come before the Court and present their cases of unanswered prayers or delayed breakthroughs to the Righteous Judge.

In this completely updated edition featuring all new material, Robert presents fresh biblical insights and a systematic framework that shows all believers how to enter the Courts of Heaven. In addition, Robert answers common questions about the Courts and reveals how this place in the spirit is available to all believers through Jesus' blood.

God's passion is to answer your prayers. When you learn how to operate in the Courts of Heaven, you can undo the spiritual legalities that stand in the way of your answered prayer. Get ready for miraculous results!

Purchase your copy wherever books are sold